Conquering Phobias

A Step-By-Step Guide to Overcoming Your Deepest Fears

Michelle Mann

Copyright © 2024 by Michelle Mann

All rights reserved.

No portion of this book may be reproduced in any form without written permission from the publisher or author, except as permitted by U.S. copyright law.

Contents

1. Introduction — 1
2. Understanding Phobias — 6
3. Preparing for the Journey — 26
4. Behavioral Techniques — 49
5. Taking Charge of the Journey — 60
6. Cognitive Strategies — 69
7. Coping Mechanisms and Techniques — 80
8. Advanced Coping Strategies — 100
9. Maintaining Progress — 110
10. Living Without Fear — 115
11. Conclusion — 121

Chapter One

Introduction

If you have a phobia, you aren't alone. Millions of people deal with phobia, and everyone deals with fear. It's normal to sometimes be afraid. The problem comes when your fear rules your life and doesn't allow you to engage fully in your own life. Phobias can be debilitating, but they don't have to be when you take charge of your mind and your life.

The prevalence of phobias varies significantly around the world, reflecting a complex interplay of cultural, societal, and individual factors. Estimates suggest that specific phobias, which encompass fears of particular objects or situations, affect a substantial portion of the global population, with figures ranging from 7% to 9% according to the World Health Organization. However, it is important to acknowledge that the reported prevalence can differ across countries and regions due to cultural nuances and varying attitudes toward mental health. There is still a significant stigma around mental health conditions, even though increased knowledge of mental disorders has started to reduce that stigma. Many cases of phobias go unreported and untreated.

Social anxiety disorder, a common form of phobia characterized by an overwhelming fear of social situations, presents prevalence rates ranging from 2% to 13%. This phobia is one of the most prevalent mental health struggles of any, showing how normal these disorders are. These figures highlight the widespread nature of phobias, emphasizing the need for a comprehensive understanding of the factors influencing their occurrence and the development of targeted interventions to address these often debilitating mental health conditions on a global scale.

Although they are common, most people misunderstand the nuanced nature of phobias. Phobias, often dismissed as silly and irrational fears, can cast a profound shadow over an individual's life, transforming routine activities into daunting challenges. These intense and irrational fears, classified as anxiety disorders, have the potential to permeate various facets of daily existence, impairing personal relationships, hindering career advancements, and limiting overall quality of life.

From the seemingly mundane to essential parts of life, phobias can trigger debilitating anxiety, leading individuals to rearrange their lives in an attempt to avoid encountering their deepest fears. People with phobias are commonly ruled by their phobias, and they feel as though they are in the passenger seat of their own lives, while their phobias are behind the wheel. It can feel hopeless when you have a phobia, and you may wonder if it's possible to ever take your life back. You can, but first you have to take some steps to learn how phobias work and what steps you must take to defeat them.

Understanding the impact of phobias is crucial, as it sheds light on the intricate ways in which these paralyzing anxieties can subvert a person's well-being and autonomy, transforming the pursuit of a fulfilling life into a relentless battle against irrational dread. The importance of addressing and managing these fears to reclaim a sense of normalcy and balance in life cannot be understated.

The book covers a range of topics that will help you understand you or your loved one's phobia and learn to take on the fear that often feels like it controls your life, making it hard for you to do all the things you love.

This book will help you in the following areas:

Understanding the Unseen Foe: This book is an exploration into the intricate terrain of phobias, those unseen foes that lurk in the recesses of our minds. It delves deep into the psychology behind these fears, unraveling the intricate tapestry of thoughts and emotions that give rise to phobias. Through self-assessment and reflection, readers are invited to identify and dissect the roots of their anxieties, laying the foundation for a personalized roadmap to recovery.

Preparing for the Odyssey: As we embark on this odyssey to conquer phobias, preparation becomes key. Building a robust support system, setting realistic goals, and understanding the various dimensions of phobia treatment become the compass points for the journey. The initial chapters act as guides, equipping readers with the tools and insights necessary to navigate the path ahead. It won't be an easy journey, but with some careful preparation, you'll be ready to face the uncomfortable feelings that perpetuate your phobia.

Behavioral Techniques: The Stepping Stones: The journey unfolds with the exploration of behavioral techniques, with exposure therapy and systematic desensitization at the forefront. These sections illuminate the process of unmasking fears, one step at a time, and empower individuals to confront their anxieties in a controlled and systematic manner. By changing your behavior, you can change your relationship with your fears and learn to overcome your phobia.

Cognitive Strategies: Illuminating the Mind's Pathways: The narrative then turns to the realm of cognitive strategies, exposing the culprits behind irrational fears—cognitive distortions. Readers are guided through the process of recognizing and challenging these distortions, setting the stage for a transformative shift in mindset. The power of positive thinking becomes a beacon, lighting the way toward the next phase of the journey. You can unpack the power of your own mind and learn that you have more control over your thoughts than you thought.

Coping Mechanisms and Techniques: Tools for Immediate Relief: The book unveils a repertoire of coping mechanisms and techniques designed to provide both immediate relief and long-term resilience. The process of recovery can feel overwhelming, but when you learn coping mechanisms, you can survive the hardest parts of recovery. From relaxation techniques like deep breathing to the transformative practice of mindfulness, readers are equipped with a holistic toolkit to navigate the challenges posed by phobias.

Advanced Coping Strategies: Elevating the Journey: The Odyssey reaches new heights with the introduction of advanced coping strategies. Visualization, imagery, hypnotherapy, and Neuro-Linguistic Programming (NLP) emerge as potent tools, offering individuals the means to transcend the boundaries of their fears and envision a life free from phobic constraints. These strategies are not always the first line of treatment, but they have proven themselves effective in a holistic process toward recovery.

Maintaining Progress: Navigating Setbacks and Forging Ahead: Acknowledging the reality of setbacks, the book provides strategies for resilience and tips for the long-term management of phobias. Real-life stories of triumph serve as beacons of hope, demonstrating that setbacks can be stepping stones toward greater strength.

Living Without Fear: A New Beginning: As the journey nears its conclusion, the focus shifts to envisioning a life unencumbered by fear. Real-life success stories inspire readers to pay it forward, reinforcing their progress through the act of teaching. The concluding chapters invite readers to embrace the possibilities, draw strength from the stories shared, and find the courage to live a life liberated from the grip of irrational fears.

Your Journey Awaits: This book is not just a collection of words on pages but a companion in your pursuit of conquering phobias. With each turn of the page, you will find not only guidance but empowerment, discovering the resilience within to live a life liberated from the shadows of fear. The odyssey toward a future without fear awaits, and the first steps are yours to take. May this book be a lantern lighting the path forward, illuminating the journey to reclaim the reins of your existence.

It's time to dive into the process of phobia recovery because there's no need to wait another day to reach for the change you so desperately want and need to have a fulfilling and content life.

Chapter Two

Understanding Phobias

Phobias are like enigmatic monsters that lurk in the shadows of the human psyche, casting their long-reaching tendrils over the daily lives of sufferers. From common fears like heights or snakes to niche fears like the color yellow, phobias manifest in myriad forms, affecting individuals across cultures, ages, and backgrounds. Phobias are complex for sufferers, it is crucial to unravel the layers that create these intense and often overwhelming fears. No matter your phobia or phobias, you can learn a lot about how to proceed by simply starting to understand your phobias and demystifying why they exist.

What are Phobias?

Phobias are intense, irrational fears that trigger severe anxiety responses in individuals, often leading to avoidance behaviors. While fear is a natural and adaptive response to perceived threats, phobias transcend the bounds of normal apprehension. These deep-seated anxieties are characterized by their irrationality, persistence, and disproportionate impact on daily life.

Before you can understand phobias, you have to understand the differences between normal fears and phobias. We all have normal fears, and fear is an imperative part of human survival. However, we do not all have phobias, and phobias are a sign that you aren't responding to the world around you in a healthy or productive way. Phobias and normal fears are distinct in terms of intensity, duration, and impact on daily life. While both are natural responses to perceived threats, they differ significantly in their manifestations and the degree to which they interfere with a person's well-being.

Phobias:

- Intensity: Phobias are characterized by an intense and irrational fear that is disproportionate to the actual threat posed by the feared object or situation. The emotional response triggered by a phobic stimulus is often overwhelming and can lead to panic attacks.

- Duration: Phobias are persistent, lasting for at least six months or longer. Unlike common fears that may dissipate over time or with exposure, phobias tend to persist and may worsen without intervention.

- Impact on Daily Life: Phobias can significantly impact a person's daily life, leading to avoidance behaviors. Individuals with phobias may go to great lengths to evade situations or objects that trigger their anxiety, affecting personal relationships, career opportunities, and overall quality of life.

- Irrationality: Phobias are irrational fears, meaning they are not always grounded in logical or realistic threats. The fear response is often out of proportion to any actual danger, and individuals with phobias are aware that their fear is excessive.

Normal Fears:

- Proportionality: Normal fears are typically proportionate to the perceived threat. For example, feeling uneasy during a thunderstorm or when encountering a wild animal is a normal fear response that aligns with the potential danger present in those situations.

- Adaptiveness: Normal fears serve an adaptive purpose, helping individuals navigate and respond to genuine threats in their environment. They are part of the natural fight-or-flight response and can contribute to survival.

- Transient Nature: Normal fears are often transient and tend to diminish over time or with repeated exposure. For instance, someone may initially feel nervous about public speaking but may become more comfortable with practice.

- Limited Impact: While normal fears can cause discomfort or anxiety, they typically do not severely interfere with daily life. Individuals can usually manage normal fears without significant disruption to their routines or relationships.

In summary, the key distinctions between phobias and normal fears lie in the intensity, duration, impact on daily life, and the rationality of the fear response. Phobias represent an extreme form of fear that requires specialized intervention for effective management and resolution.

Phobias can manifest in various forms, from specific phobias targeting particular objects or situations, such as spiders, heights, or flying, to social phobias that induce intense anxiety in social settings. Agoraphobia, a more complex phobia, involves a fear of open spaces, crowded areas, and situations perceived as challenging to escape. The fear response in phobias is often disproportionate to the actual threat posed by the feared object or situation, so people with phobias often logically know that they are being unreasonable but cannot control their response to their phobia stimuli.

Identifying a phobia, therefore, involves recognizing the excessive and uncontrollable nature of the fear, its impact on daily life, and the presence of avoidance behaviors. Individuals with phobias often will do things that seem extreme to others to make sure they never have to encounter their fear. For example, someone who is afraid of spiders may not want to go outside at all because they are so intimidated by even the thought of seeing a spider outside.

While phobias can be debilitating, and often are, they are not insurmountable. Treatment options, ranging from therapeutic techniques like exposure therapy and cognitive restructuring to medications, offer avenues for individuals to confront and overcome their fears. Understanding the intricacies of phobias is a crucial step toward dismantling their power, paving the way for a journey from fear to freedom. At the end of the day, although phobias feel powerful, you are the one who gets the final word when it comes to how you think and behave.

Roots of Phobias

The roots of phobias are a complex interplay of genetic predispositions, traumatic experiences, and learned behaviors. Understanding these roots is crucial for developing effective strategies for treatment and management, but it's important to know that there's no easy explanation for phobias, and researchers are still trying to discover more exact reasons for phobias.

Phobias can emerge from a combination of these factors, and different individuals may have unique combinations of influences contributing to their specific fears. Treatment approaches, such as cognitive-behavioral therapy (CBT) and exposure therapy, often aim to address these roots by modifying thought patterns, desensitizing individuals to feared stimuli, and providing tools for coping with anxiety. Knowing the factors at play for your phobias will help you understand how to get the best treatment and ensure you are prepared for all the potential obstacles in your path.

Genetic Factors

Genetic factors play a significant role in the development of phobias, contributing to an individual's predisposition to anxiety and fear responses. While environmental factors and personal experiences also influence the onset of phobias, genetic components contribute to the overall susceptibility to developing these anxiety disorders.

Research suggests a hereditary component in the transmission of phobias. Individuals with a family history of anxiety disorders, including specific phobias, are more likely to exhibit similar phobic tendencies. This familial pattern indicates a genetic influence on the predisposition to heightened fear responses and the development of irrational fears, but it may also suggest certain environmental factors as well.

Specific genetic variations may impact neurotransmitter systems, such as those involving serotonin and dopamine, which play crucial roles in regulating mood and emotional responses. Variations in these genetic factors can influence an individual's vulnerability to anxiety and contribute to the manifestation of phobias. Not all people with certain genes will develop a phobia, but they will be more likely to develop a phobia at some point in their lives.

It's important to note that while genetics contribute to the risk of developing phobias, environmental factors also play a crucial role, so most of the time, genetics can only offer so much information about your situation. Traumatic experiences, conditioning, and learned behaviors can significantly influence the development and exacerbation of phobias, even in individuals with a genetic predisposition. All that is to say that anyone can have a phobia, regardless of their genes.

Brain Structure and Function

Phobias are closely linked to the structure and function of the brain, particularly involving areas responsible for processing emotions and regulating fear responses. Thus, the way your brain is designed has a huge role in your development of phobias, and it can also have just as big of a role in how you combat your phobia.

The amygdala, a small almond-shaped structure located deep within the brain's temporal lobe, plays a central role in the development and maintenance of phobias. It is responsible for processing emotional stimuli, particularly fear-inducing ones, and plays a pivotal role in the initiation of the body's "fight or flight" response. This response is one humans have all developed as a way to act quickly in situations of danger, but your brain can inadvertently engage this response even when you're not in any real danger.

In individuals with phobias, the amygdala exhibits heightened activity when exposed to the feared stimulus, triggering the release of stress hormones and initiating the physiological responses associated with fear. This hyperactivity of the amygdala contributes to the exaggerated fear response observed in phobic individuals, even in situations that pose little or no actual threat. If you're afraid of dogs, seeing a dog behind a fence may feel like you're being attacked by your amygdala, even though logically, you know that isn't accurate.

The prefrontal cortex, responsible for executive functions such as decision-making and emotional regulation, also plays a crucial role in phobias. Individuals with phobias may exhibit alterations in the functioning of the prefrontal cortex, impacting their ability to regulate emotional responses effectively. This dysregulation can contribute to the persistence of irrational fears and difficulties in overcoming phobias through rational thought processes.

Neurotransmitter systems, including those involving serotonin and gamma-aminobutyric acid (GABA), are implicated in the modulation of anxiety and fear. Variations in these neurotransmitter systems may contribute to the vulnerability to developing phobias and the intensity of fear responses.

Functional neuroimaging studies, such as fMRI (functional magnetic resonance imaging) and PET (positron emission tomography) scans, have provided valuable insights into the neural mechanisms underlying phobias, even if there is still a lot to learn about how your brain works, particularly in respect to phobias. These studies demonstrate altered patterns of brain activation and connectivity in individuals with phobias, highlighting the intricate interplay between brain structures and functions in the manifestation of irrational fears.

Understanding the neurobiological basis of phobias is essential for developing targeted therapeutic interventions. Cognitive-behavioral therapies, particularly exposure therapy, aim to recondition the brain's response to feared stimuli by gradually exposing individuals in a controlled and supportive environment. Medications that influence neurotransmitter activity may also be prescribed to modulate anxiety levels. Overall, unraveling the intricate relationship between brain structure and function in phobias informs evidence-based treatments and contributes to more effective strategies for overcoming irrational fears.

Traumatic Events and Fearful Experiences

Traumatic experiences and fearful events can easily impact a person's psyche, shaping an individual's vulnerability to irrational fears. Understanding how your traumas and other life events impact the development of phobias is crucial for devising effective therapeutic interventions and preventive strategies because traumatic events require trauma-informed care and can require you to unpack and address those specific events and not just the fear itself.

Traumatic experiences can serve as significant catalysts for the emergence of phobias. Individuals who have undergone distressing or frightening events related to specific stimuli may develop intense and persistent fears associated with those triggers. For example, a person who experienced a traumatic incident involving water may develop a phobia of swimming. The emotional imprint of such events contributes to the association of the stimuli with danger, laying the groundwork for the development of irrational fears. Not all phobias are so straightforward, however. The mind is complicated, so you may not be able to trace back your phobia to just one experience.

Classical conditioning is a fundamental psychological process that plays a significant role in the development of phobias. This type of learning occurs when a neutral stimulus becomes associated with an aversive or fear-inducing event, leading to a conditioned response even in the absence of the original threat. In the context of phobias, classical conditioning establishes a powerful link between a specific stimulus and the emotional response of fear.

For example, consider an individual who experiences a traumatic event involving a thunderstorm. The thunderstorm (neutral stimulus) becomes paired with the fear and anxiety elicited during the traumatic incident (unconditioned response). Over time, the thunderstorm transforms into a conditioned stimulus that triggers fear (conditioned response) independently of the original traumatic experience. In this way, the person develops a phobia of thunderstorms through the process of classical conditioning.

Understanding classical conditioning in phobias helps explain why seemingly neutral stimuli can provoke intense and irrational fear responses. The association formed between the conditioned stimulus and the emotional response becomes deeply ingrained, contributing to the persistence of phobic reactions. Therapeutic approaches, such as exposure therapy, aim to disrupt this learned association by gradually exposing individuals to the phobic stimulus in a controlled and supportive environment. Through systematic exposure, the goal is to recondition the individual's response, reducing the fear and anxiety associated with the once-neutral stimulus.

Preventive measures and early intervention strategies should consider the role of traumatic and fearful experiences in phobia development. Addressing and processing traumatic events, particularly through therapeutic interventions like exposure therapy, can help mitigate the impact of these experiences on the development of irrational fears. Ultimately, creating supportive environments that encourage adaptive coping mechanisms and challenge maladaptive beliefs is essential for preventing the onset and persistence of phobias. While steps can be taken to reduce the development of phobias, there is no way to guarantee that a phobia won't develop.

Environmental Factors

Environmental factors also contribute to the acquisition of phobias. Environmental cues and contextual factors that reinforce avoidance behaviors can further solidify the development and persistence of phobias. Identical twin studies show that phobias are not just influenced by a person's DNA, but they are also influenced by how and where they were raised.

Social and cultural influences within an individual's environment can impact the prevalence and nature of specific phobias. Culturally specific fears may emerge based on shared beliefs, norms, and exposure to certain stimuli. Additionally, societal messages about danger and risk can contribute to the amplification or attenuation of phobic responses. For instance, media portrayal of certain situations as threatening may influence the development of phobias related to those scenarios.

Vicarious learning, or learning through observation, is a profound pathway through which phobias can be transmitted. If individuals observe others expressing fear or avoidance behaviors in response to certain stimuli, they may internalize this information and develop similar phobic responses.

This is particularly relevant in the context of social learning, where family members, friends, or peers can serve as models for phobic behaviors, influencing an individual's perceptions and reactions. Your brain becomes whatever information is put into it, both consciously and unconsciously. Children, in particular, are susceptible to learning fears through observational experiences. If a child witnesses a parent expressing fear or avoidance toward certain stimuli, they may internalize those reactions and develop similar phobic responses.

Environmental factors contribute significantly to the etiology of phobias. Integrating these factors into therapeutic approaches and preventive interventions enhances our understanding of phobia development and allows for more targeted and holistic strategies to address these anxiety disorders.

Cognitive Factors

Cognitive factors play a crucial role in the development and maintenance of phobias, shaping the way individuals perceive and respond to fear-inducing stimuli. One significant cognitive factor is catastrophic thinking, wherein individuals anticipate the worst possible outcomes associated with their phobic triggers. This negative thought pattern intensifies anxiety and contributes to the avoidance behaviors characteristic of phobias. For instance, someone with a fear of flying may engage in catastrophic thinking, envisioning plane crashes and heightening their anxiety about air travel.

Cognitive distortions are also prevalent in phobias, involving irrational thought patterns that contribute to the persistence of fears. Overgeneralization, where individuals draw broad conclusions based on limited experiences, and magnification, where they exaggerate the significance or threat level of their phobic triggers, are common cognitive distortions. These distortions contribute to the perceived danger of the phobic stimulus, reinforcing avoidance behaviors and maintaining the irrational fear.

Selective attention, a cognitive process, further influences phobias as individuals tend to focus disproportionately on their feared stimuli. This attentional bias reinforces the perception of threat, making it challenging for individuals with phobias to shift their focus away from the source of their fear. Cognitive-behavioral therapy often targets these attentional biases, helping individuals redirect their focus and challenge irrational thought patterns.

Personality Traits

Personality traits can significantly influence an individual's susceptibility to developing phobias, shaping their emotional responses and coping mechanisms in the face of fear-inducing stimuli.

One prominent personality trait linked to phobias is neuroticism. Individuals with high neuroticism levels tend to experience heightened emotional reactivity and anxiety, making them more prone to developing persistent and irrational fears. The inclination towards negative emotions and a tendency to overreact emotionally may contribute to the intensification of phobic reactions, influencing the severity and persistence of specific fears.

Behavioral inhibition, another personality trait, is also relevant in phobias. Individuals with a strong tendency towards behavioral inhibition often exhibit a cautious and avoidant approach to novel or challenging situations. This avoidance behavior can contribute to the development and maintenance of phobias, as individuals may seek to escape situations that trigger their anxieties. The cautious temperament associated with high levels of behavioral inhibition may lead to a narrowing of experiences and hinder adaptive coping strategies.

Conscientiousness, a personality trait characterized by self-discipline and responsibility, may also be relevant to the development of phobias. Lower levels of conscientiousness, marked by impulsivity and a lack of self-control, may be associated with an increased risk of developing specific phobias. Impulsive individuals may engage in avoidance behaviors without thoroughly considering the consequences, potentially reinforcing their irrational fears. Contrarily, some people with phobias can be overly conscientious, leading them to not wanting to take any risks.

While the relationship between openness to experience and phobias is less straightforward, certain sub-types within openness, such as heightened sensitivity to novel stimuli, may influence an individual's predisposition to phobias. Those with greater openness may be more receptive to novel fears but may also exhibit a greater capacity for exploring therapeutic interventions that involve exposure to feared stimuli. Just like people, the personality traits of those with phobias can have a lot of overlap but also a lot of diversity.

Identifying Phobias

Identifying if you have a phobia involves recognizing persistent and disproportionate fears that extend beyond normal apprehensions. Take note of situations or objects that consistently trigger intense anxiety, leading to physical symptoms like a rapid heartbeat, sweating, trembling, or nausea. If these reactions are disproportionate to the actual threat posed by the situation and persist for at least six months or more, it may indicate a phobia.

Additionally, observe your behaviors – if you actively avoid specific situations or objects due to fear and find that this avoidance significantly impacts your daily life, relationships, or activities, it could be indicative of a phobia. Self-reflection is essential; consider the duration, frequency, and intensity of your fears to determine if they align with the diagnostic criteria for phobias.

Engaging in self-assessment tools or questionnaires designed to identify phobias can provide valuable insights. Online resources often offer checklists and quizzes to help individuals evaluate their fears and potential phobic reactions. Seeking feedback from trusted friends, family members, or colleagues can offer an external perspective on your behaviors and emotional responses.

However, a conclusive diagnosis should be made by a mental health professional who can conduct a thorough assessment, considering various factors such as your personal history, symptoms, and the impact of fears on your daily life. If you suspect you have a phobia, reaching out to a mental health professional is a crucial step toward accurate identification and the development of an appropriate treatment plan.

If you are concerned about a loved one, urge them to get the help they need and support them on that journey.

Phobia Types and Diagnosis

Phobias are classified under anxiety disorders in the Diagnostic and Statistical Manual of Mental Disorders, Fifth Edition (DSM-5), which is widely used by mental health professionals for diagnostic purposes. There are three primary types of phobias outlined in the DSM-5:

Specific Phobia

Specific phobias are a type of anxiety disorders characterized by an intense and irrational fear of specific objects, situations, or activities. Individuals with specific phobias experience overwhelming anxiety and distress when exposed to their feared stimuli, which can include animals, heights, flying, needles, and various environmental elements. Unlike common fears that may cause discomfort but are manageable, specific phobias lead to avoidance behaviors, where individuals go to great lengths to evade the source of their fear. This avoidance can significantly impact their daily lives, limiting their activities and social interactions.

The onset of specific phobias is often linked to a traumatic experience or a learned behavioral response, and they tend to persist without intervention. Although individuals with specific phobias may recognize that their fear is excessive or irrational, the emotional response can be challenging to control. The anticipation of encountering the feared object or situation can trigger intense anxiety, leading to physical symptoms such as sweating, trembling, increased heart rate, and, in extreme cases, panic attacks.

Social Anxiety Disorder (Social Phobia)

Social phobia, also known as social anxiety disorder, is a mental health condition characterized by an overwhelming and persistent fear of social situations where an individual may be exposed to scrutiny or judgment. People with social phobia often experience intense anxiety and distress in various social contexts, such as public speaking, meeting new people, or participating in group activities. The fear is not merely a discomfort in social situations but is marked by a profound concern about being embarrassed, humiliated, or negatively evaluated by others.

Individuals with social phobia may go to great lengths to avoid social situations that trigger their anxiety, impacting their personal, academic, and professional lives. This avoidance behavior can lead to isolation and may hinder the development of meaningful relationships and the pursuit of personal and professional goals. Social phobia can manifest in physical symptoms such as trembling, sweating, blushing, and an elevated heart rate, reflecting the physiological arousal associated with the fear response.

Agoraphobia

Agoraphobia is a complex anxiety disorder characterized by an intense fear of situations or places where escape might be difficult or help is unavailable, leading to feelings of panic and extreme discomfort. Individuals with agoraphobia often avoid places such as crowded spaces, public transportation, shopping malls, or any location perceived as challenging to leave swiftly. The fear is not solely about the place itself but is driven by concerns about experiencing a panic attack or another incapacitating event in that setting.

This anxiety disorder can significantly impact a person's daily life, limiting their ability to engage in routine activities that many others take for granted. Many people struggle to leave their houses or small safe areas. Agoraphobia often develops as a response to a previous panic attack or other traumatic experiences, and the fear tends to generalize to various environments. Individuals with agoraphobia may go to great lengths to avoid triggering situations, resulting in social isolation and hindering their overall quality of life.

While agoraphobia can be debilitating, early intervention and appropriate treatment strategies empower individuals to regain control over their lives and confront the challenges associated with this anxiety disorder.

Across Phobias

For each type of phobia, the DSM-5 criteria emphasize that the fear or anxiety is excessive or unreasonable and significantly interferes with the individual's daily life and functioning. Diagnosis should be made by a qualified mental health professional based on a thorough clinical assessment, including interviews, observations, and consideration of the individual's specific symptoms and history. However, most people will be able to self-identify if they have a phobia and can easily relate to the symptoms.

Fear Response and Phobias

The fear response is a fundamental and adaptive aspect of human physiology, designed to alert individuals to potential threats and activate the body's "fight or flight" mechanisms. In the context of phobias, however, this natural response becomes exaggerated and disproportionate, leading to intense and irrational fear in response to specific stimuli. The fear response involves the activation of the autonomic nervous system, triggering a cascade of physiological changes aimed at preparing the body to confront or escape from a perceived danger.

In individuals with phobias, the fear response is often triggered by situations or objects that, in reality, pose little or no actual threat. This heightened response can manifest through various symptoms, including increased heart rate, rapid breathing, sweating, trembling, and a strong desire to avoid the feared stimulus.

Through systematic desensitization, individuals can learn to manage and eventually overcome their irrational fears, fostering a more balanced and adaptive response to situations that once incited overwhelming anxiety. This recalibration of the fear response is a key element in the journey toward conquering phobias and reclaiming a sense of control over one's emotional well-being.

Diagnosis of Phobias

Diagnosing phobias involves a comprehensive assessment by mental health professionals to understand the nature and impact of an individual's fears. Many people are scared to be assessed because they don't know what to expect, which can cause heightened anxiety. While each professional will approach diagnosis differently, you can expect certain similarities.

The process typically includes the following components:

Clinical Evaluation: Mental health professionals, such as psychologists or psychiatrists, conduct a clinical evaluation to gather detailed information about the individual's symptoms, experiences, and overall mental health. This may involve discussing the specific phobic triggers, the duration and intensity of the fear response, and how it affects daily life.

Diagnostic Criteria: Phobias are diagnosed based on specific criteria outlined in the Diagnostic and Statistical Manual of Mental Disorders (DSM-5), a widely used classification system for mental health conditions. For a diagnosis of a specific phobia, criteria include experiencing intense fear or anxiety triggered by a specific object or situation, actively avoiding the feared stimulus, and the fear causing significant distress or impairment in daily functioning.

Self-Reporting and Observation: Individuals are often asked to self-report their experiences, providing insights into the subjective distress caused by their phobia. Additionally, mental health professionals may observe the individual's reactions in relevant situations to better understand the severity of the phobia and its impact on their lives. Logs are often used to help with self-reporting.

Differential Diagnosis: Mental health professionals conduct a differential diagnosis to rule out other potential causes of the symptoms. This process helps ensure that the diagnosed condition accurately reflects the individual's experiences and is not a result of another underlying mental health issue. Some physical conditions or other mental disorders can cause similar symptoms, and those issues may need to be ruled out before the professional can confidently give a diagnosis.

Assessment Tools and Questionnaires: Psychological assessments, questionnaires, and standardized tools may be employed to gather quantitative data about the phobia. These tools help assess the severity of the phobia, its impact on daily functioning, and any coexisting conditions that may be present. These tools can seem stressful, but they are given in a non-judgmental manner.

Collaborative Approach: The diagnostic process is often collaborative, involving open communication between the individual and the mental health professional. It is crucial for individuals to share their experiences openly, providing accurate information that aids in a precise diagnosis and the development of an effective treatment plan. You are a part of the recovery process, so you get to make decisions about how you want to go about recovering.

Chapter Three

Preparing for the Journey

Embarking on the journey to overcome phobias can be an arduous task, but it becomes considerably more manageable and empowering with a robust support system in place. In this chapter, we delve into the profound importance of building a support network during the treatment of phobias. From defining what a support network entails to understanding how it facilitates the recovery process, we explore the diverse roles friends, family, coworkers, spiritual community members, support groups, and internet communities play. Additionally, we provide practical guidance on how individuals can proactively build and strengthen their support systems for sustained progress and triumph over phobias.

Creating a Support System

Embarking on the journey to overcome phobias can be an arduous task, but it becomes considerably more manageable and empowering with a robust support system in place. In this chapter, we delve into the profound importance of building a support network during the treatment of phobias. From defining what a support network entails to understanding how it facilitates the recovery process, we explore the diverse roles friends, family, coworkers, spiritual community members, support groups, and internet communities play. Additionally, we provide practical guidance on how individuals can proactively build and strengthen their support systems for sustained progress and triumph over phobias.

Defining a Support Network

A support network is an interconnected web of individuals who provide emotional, practical, and sometimes even financial assistance to someone facing challenges. In the context of phobia treatment, this network becomes a crucial foundation for emotional well-being, offering understanding, empathy, and encouragement. It extends beyond familial and friendship circles to encompass various communities that can contribute to an individual's mental and emotional resilience. Having a support network allows you to use your emotional and physical resources more wisely. Humans are social creatures, so we all need some level of support to ensure overall well-being.

The Role of a Support Network in Phobia Recovery

A support network serves as a safety net, catching individuals during moments of vulnerability and providing the encouragement needed to persevere through challenges. It offers a sense of belonging, understanding, and shared experience, which can be especially comforting for those grappling with the isolating nature of phobias. The network not only aids in navigating the treatment process but also becomes a source of motivation, fostering a belief in one's ability to overcome fears. Feeling alone can make it hard to overcome a phobia, making you feel like you are unusual or unwelcome in the "normal" world.

Types of Support

Social support is crucial for individuals dealing with phobias, but there isn't just one kind of support that people seek when they are trying to transform their lives. Most people need multiple avenues of support to get through their healing journeys effectively. Here are different types of social support that can be beneficial:

Emotional Support

Emotional support involves expressing empathy, care, love, and understanding toward the individual with a phobia. Friends and family provide a comforting presence during anxiety-inducing situations, offering words of encouragement, and being understanding about the challenges the person faces. Emotional support is one of the most important kinds of support when it comes to recovering from phobias because phobias can be so emotionally draining.

Instrumental Support

Instrumental support entails tangible assistance and practical help in managing daily tasks affected by the phobia. Friends or family members assisting with logistical aspects, such as accompanying the person during exposure therapy sessions, helping with transportation, or aiding in specific tasks related to their phobia. It relieves a huge burden when you don't have to worry about every little detail of your recovery. Even little things like giving you a meal after a hard session can be incredibly useful.

Informational Support

Informational support involves providing knowledge and guidance about the phobia, treatment options, and coping strategies. Friends or family members researching and sharing information about the specific phobia, its triggers, and effective therapeutic interventions. They may also accompany the individual to appointments with mental health professionals and help them process information that those professionals offer.

Appraisal Support

Appraisal support includes constructive feedback, encouragement, and positive reinforcement regarding the individual's efforts to manage and overcome their phobia. Friends acknowledge the person's progress, praising their courage during exposure exercises, and providing positive reinforcement for steps taken toward facing their fears. Sometimes, it is hard for you to see your own progress unless you have someone reminding you that you have made progress.

Companionship

Companionship involves being physically present and offering a sense of togetherness, particularly during challenging situations. Friends or family members accompany the individual to events or places that trigger their phobia, providing a supportive presence and helping to alleviate feelings of isolation. Sometimes, companionship is just about being there for a person. You don't even have to talk about the phobia, and distraction can be a useful technique for people struggling to get their minds off phobic thoughts.

Validation

Validation support entails acknowledging the individual's feelings and experiences without judgment, reinforcing the legitimacy of their emotions. Friends or family members validate the person's fears, recognizing the difficulty they face, and expressing understanding without minimizing or dismissing their concerns. The goal of validation is not to encourage the person's phobias, but it is to validate that dealing with phobias is hard and can feel incredibly scary.

Social Integration

Social integration involves facilitating the person's involvement in social activities and events to promote a sense of belonging. Friends encourage the individual to participate in group activities or events, creating opportunities for social interactions that contribute to a supportive and inclusive environment. Many people with phobias isolate themselves, so social integration helps them open themselves to enjoyable experiences they may not normally have.

Networking

Networking support involves connecting the individual with others who may share similar experiences or providing access to relevant resources. Friends or family members connecting the person with support groups, online communities, or mental health professionals who specialize in treating specific phobias.

By encompassing these various types of social support, individuals with phobias can benefit from a comprehensive network that addresses their emotional, practical, and informational needs, fostering a conducive environment for healing and growth.

Components of a Support Network

There are many people that can make up a support network, and each type of person will have a specific role in the recovery process.

Friends

Friends, with their shared history and mutual understanding, often form the frontline of a support network. Their role involves offering companionship, encouragement, and practical assistance, creating a sense of normalcy during the recovery journey.

Family

Family members, bound by blood or chosen, provide unconditional love and support. Their constant presence becomes a pillar of strength, offering stability and reassurance during moments of distress.

Coworkers

For many, coworkers represent a significant portion of their daily life. A supportive work environment can contribute positively to phobia recovery. Coworkers can offer understanding, create a supportive workplace, and assist in managing stressors related to work. Because your phobia can impact work, it can be imperative to have support in your workplace.

Spiritual Community Members

For individuals with a spiritual inclination, spiritual and religious communities become an essential aspect of their support network. Shared beliefs and values provide a unique source of comfort, fostering a sense of purpose and connection.

Support Groups

Formal support groups bring together individuals facing similar challenges, creating a space for shared experiences and empathy. Whether in-person or online, these groups provide a platform for individuals to learn from one another, offer encouragement, and combat the isolation that often accompanies phobias.

Internet Communities

In the digital age, internet communities offer a convenient avenue for support. Online forums, social media groups, and dedicated platforms enable individuals to connect with others facing similar challenges globally, breaking down geographical barriers and providing a diverse array of perspectives.

Building an Effective Support Network

You may know the type of people that you want to support you, but knowing how to begin the process of effectively using your support network can feel overwhelming if you don't have a support network already in place. With a few easy steps, you can start building an effective support network.

Facilitate

Open and Honest Communication

Individuals dealing with phobias play a fundamental role in promoting open and honest communication within their support system. By openly expressing their thoughts, fears, and needs, they provide crucial insights that enable their support network to better understand the nature of their phobia and the challenges they face. Initiating conversations about specific triggers, boundaries, and coping mechanisms fosters a shared understanding, laying the groundwork for a supportive environment.

Encouraging transparent communication also involves expressing expectations from the support system. Whether it's the need for emotional reassurance, practical assistance, or collaborative participation in exposure exercises, individuals with phobias can articulate the type of support that is most beneficial for them. This proactive communication empowers their support network to align their efforts with the specific needs of the individual, contributing to a more effective and empathetic support system.

By actively participating in collaborative problem-solving, individuals with phobias contribute to a dynamic support system that adapts to their evolving needs. Celebrating successes, no matter how small, reinforces positive progress and encourages continued efforts. This ongoing communication loop promotes a culture of continuous learning within the support system, fostering an atmosphere where everyone feels heard, valued, and committed to the collective journey of overcoming phobias. In essence, individuals with phobias serve as catalysts for open and honest communication, creating a resilient support network that enhances their capacity to navigate and conquer their fears.

Establishing Boundaries

For individuals grappling with phobias, establishing and communicating boundaries is a vital aspect of navigating daily life while prioritizing mental well-being. Setting boundaries involves a thoughtful process of self-reflection to identify specific triggers and comfort levels. These boundaries may encompass particular situations, environments, or behaviors that could exacerbate anxiety associated with the phobia. Communicating these boundaries openly is key, using assertive "I" statements to express needs without placing blame. Educating those in one's support network about the nature of the phobia helps foster understanding, emphasizing the importance of respect for established boundaries.

Creating realistic expectations ensures that the boundaries set are both achievable and reflective of the individual's comfort level. In this process, a support plan can be developed collaboratively, outlining strategies for managing challenging situations and providing a safety net for the individual. Utilizing non-verbal cues or signals becomes essential, especially in situations where verbal communication may be challenging, such as crowded environments. Establishing consequences for crossing boundaries is a crucial element, clearly communicated to reinforce the significance of respecting these limits.

Positive reinforcement plays a role, acknowledging and praising supportive behavior from the network when boundaries are respected. Regular check-ins with the support system help maintain open communication, ensuring that everyone remains aware of evolving needs and making any necessary adjustments to the established boundaries. Seeking professional guidance, when needed, further enhances the understanding of the challenges associated with phobias and reinforces the importance of respecting the individual's boundaries. Ultimately, setting and maintaining boundaries is an ongoing process that empowers individuals with phobias to navigate their daily lives with a sense of control and support.

Reciprocity in Relationships

Reciprocity in relationships plays a crucial role in supporting individuals with phobias as they navigate the challenges posed by their fears. In the context of phobias, reciprocity involves a mutual understanding and exchange of support between the individual and their network. People with phobias often rely on their relationships for emotional and practical support, and reciprocating this support fosters a dynamic where both parties feel valued and understood.

Reciprocity manifests in various forms, including emotional reassurance, active participation in exposure exercises, and the creation of a supportive environment. Those in the support network offer empathy and understanding, acknowledging the unique struggles associated with phobias. In return, individuals with phobias express gratitude and reciprocate by actively engaging in their therapeutic journey, taking steps to manage their fears, and contributing to a positive and collaborative atmosphere.

Mutual respect for established boundaries is a key aspect of reciprocity. The support network respects the individual's needs and triggers, creating a safe space for them to navigate their phobias. In turn, individuals with phobias communicate openly about their experiences, ensuring that their support system is informed and empowered to provide the necessary assistance.

Reciprocal relationships contribute to a sense of balance and shared responsibility. As individuals with phobias work toward overcoming their fears, their support network becomes an integral part of the journey. By acknowledging and reciprocating the support they receive, individuals with phobias strengthen their relationships, creating a foundation of understanding, trust, and shared progress. Ultimately, reciprocity in relationships for people with phobias cultivates an environment where everyone involved feels supported, valued, and empowered in the collective effort towards overcoming challenges associated with phobias.

Diversifying Support Sources

Diversifying support sources is a valuable strategy for individuals dealing with phobias, as it enhances the resilience of their support network and ensures a comprehensive approach to managing their fears. Relying on a variety of sources can provide different perspectives, coping strategies, and forms of assistance.

Firstly, diversification within personal relationships is essential. While family and friends may offer emotional support, consider including peers who may share similar experiences with phobias. Support groups, both in-person and online, provide a platform for connecting with individuals facing similar challenges, fostering a sense of community and understanding.

Expanding support to professional sources is equally crucial. Mental health professionals, including psychologists, counselors, and therapists, bring specialized knowledge and therapeutic interventions to help individuals manage and overcome phobias. Seeking advice from multiple professionals, each with their expertise, can enrich the therapeutic journey.

Utilizing community resources is another way to diversify support. Local mental health organizations, workshops, or community centers may offer programs specifically designed for individuals dealing with phobias. These resources can provide additional tools and strategies to complement individualized treatment plans.

Moreover, considering alternative therapies or self-help resources broadens the spectrum of support. Techniques such as mindfulness, meditation, or holistic approaches can complement traditional therapeutic methods, providing individuals with additional tools for managing anxiety associated with phobias.

Diversifying support sources not only ensures a more robust network but also increases the likelihood of discovering approaches and insights that resonate with the individual's unique needs. It empowers individuals with phobias to build a comprehensive toolkit for managing their fears, fostering resilience, and creating a more adaptable support system.

Support You Can Count On

Building a strong support system is not just a beneficial addition to phobia recovery; it's a vital component of the journey towards liberation. Friends, family, coworkers, spiritual community members, support groups, and internet communities collectively form a safety net, offering understanding, encouragement, and shared strength. As individuals navigate the complexities of phobia treatment, a well-constructed support network becomes a guiding force, illuminating the path towards triumph and a life free from the shackles of irrational fears.

Getting Professional Help

Recovering from phobias is a journey marked by resilience, self-discovery, and the courage to confront deep-seated fears. While a robust support system plays a critical role, there are instances where seeking professional help becomes a beacon of guidance and a crucial companion on the path to healing. This exploration delves into the nuances of finding the right mental health professional, understanding the need for specialization, and embracing diverse treatment approaches tailored to address the intricacies of phobias.

Recognizing the Value of Professional Help

In the intricate landscape of phobias, seeking professional help is not a sign of weakness but a testament to one's commitment to personal growth and well-being. While some people may be able to take on their phobias alone, many people will want to have some level of professional support. Phobias often have roots that go beyond the surface, intertwining with complex psychological factors that may necessitate professional intervention. Acknowledging this need is the first step towards a more nuanced and targeted approach to recovery, and professionals are detached sources who can help people figure out the complexities of their battle with phobias.

The prevalence of seeking professional support for phobias is higher than one might think. Many individuals grappling with phobias find solace and effective solutions through therapeutic interventions. The realization that seeking professional help is a common and constructive step can alleviate any stigma or hesitation surrounding the decision.

Types of Mental Health Professionals

When seeking professional help for phobias, individuals have several options to consider. Psychologists, psychiatrists, counselors, and therapists are among the primary providers of mental health support, each bringing unique qualifications and approaches to the table.

- Psychologists: Psychologists are trained in psychological assessment, diagnosis, and treatment. They may specialize in various therapeutic modalities, such as cognitive-behavioral therapy (CBT), exposure therapy, or mindfulness-based interventions, tailored to address specific phobias.

- Psychiatrists: Psychiatrists are medical doctors specialized in the diagnosis, treatment, and prevention of mental health disorders. They are licensed to prescribe medication, which may be beneficial for individuals with severe phobias or co-occurring mental health conditions.

- Counselors and Therapists: Counselors and therapists often hold master's degrees in counseling or related fields and are trained to provide counseling and psychotherapy. They may specialize in specific areas, such as anxiety disorders, and employ various therapeutic techniques to address phobias.

Expectations in Treatment for Phobias

For those grappling with phobias, understanding what to expect from treatment is crucial. The therapeutic journey often involves a gradual process of exposure, cognitive restructuring, and the development of coping mechanisms. Having realistic expectations empowers individuals to actively engage in their treatment with confidence and commitment.

The main thing you need to remember is that treatment is not a magic solution, and it won't have instantaneous results. Treatment takes time, and it can take months or years for people with phobias to see the results they want. Gradual change doesn't mean that change doesn't happen, but when you have deeply entrenched issues, it's expected that it will take time to address those issues and start to make meaningful changes. Often, those who have phobias for longer or more severely will require greater efforts to overcome those phobias, but how long treatment will take will depend on the specifics of your case.

Navigating the Process

When you're navigating the process, it can be incredibly overwhelming, and you may not be sure how you should go about getting the treatment you need. Fortunately, there are clear steps you can take to get on path that helps you recover and heal. These steps are not a requirement, and you can decide which ones are right for you, but they are an easy way to promote efficiency in your phobia treatment and lessen the emotional burden of starting treatment.

Initiating the Search

The process of finding the right mental health professional begins with a deliberate and informed search. Online directories, referrals from primary care physicians, and recommendations from friends or support groups are valuable starting points. Getting started is often the hardest step because people commonly put this step off. The best option is to take this step as soon as you get a chance. The longer you wait, the longer you delay your recovery.

Assessing Compatibility

Choosing the right mental health professional is a critical decision that can significantly impact the success of treatment for phobias. Several factors should be considered when making this choice, including:

- Specialization: Look for professionals who have experience and expertise in treating phobias specifically. Specialization in anxiety disorders or exposure therapy can be particularly beneficial. You may have to verify this experience during an initial appointment because some therapists say they work with certain issues without having extensive experience in dealing with those issues.

- Approach: Consider the therapeutic approach and techniques used by the professional. Cognitive-behavioral therapy (CBT), exposure therapy, and mindfulness-based interventions are among the evidence-based approaches commonly used to treat phobias. Different approaches work for different people, so while one approach may be "evidence-based," you may find that it doesn't work well for you and can try other methods.

Once potential professionals are identified, assessing compatibility becomes crucial. Personal compatibility and rapport with the mental health professional are essential for building a trusting therapeutic relationship. Consider factors such as communication style, cultural sensitivity, and shared values when evaluating compatibility.

An initial consultation or conversation can provide insights into the professional's approach, communication style, and overall demeanor. A sense of comfort and trust is fundamental for a fruitful therapeutic relationship. The right person for you is very individual, so it's good to reach out to multiple practitioners if possible so you can get a better sense of who they are and whether you connect with them. If you don't find someone the first time, that doesn't mean you won't find someone who works well for you. Finding a good mental health professional can be a lot like finding a good friend, so while someone may come highly recommended, that doesn't mean that they will fit with your personal needs.

Financial Considerations

Considering the financial aspects of therapy is practical and responsible, especially because it can be expensive for many people. While financial considerations are a huge part of any mental health care, even if you don't have a great financial situation, don't assume that you won't be able to get the mental health care you need to thrive despite your phobias.

Understanding insurance coverage, exploring sliding scale options, or discussing payment plans with professionals can help make mental health support more accessible. You may also be able to find sponsorship programs that help people with phobias find professionals that can help them.

One essential step is to thoroughly review your health insurance policy to understand the extent of mental health coverage it offers. Contacting your insurance provider for details on copayments, coverage limits, and any pre-authorization requirements is crucial for informed decision-making.

If you are employed, consider exploring your company's Employee Assistance Program (EAP), which often provides counseling services for mental health issues. EAP services are typically offered at reduced or no cost and may provide short-term counseling or referrals to specialists.

Additionally, inquire about sliding scale fees from mental health professionals based on income. Many therapists and clinics offer this option, making treatment more affordable for individuals with financial constraints. This type of treatment may limit the professionals who will work with you, but advocating for yourself and seeking the best benefits will improve your odds of success.

Nonprofit organizations dedicated to mental health may also offer resources or assistance in finding affordable treatment options. Online and in-person support groups can provide valuable insights and advice for managing mental health challenges while fostering a sense of community. Telehealth services, which offer therapy sessions through video calls, can be a cost-effective and convenient alternative to traditional in-person therapy.

Explore government assistance programs in your area that may provide mental health services at reduced costs. Some regions have public mental health services specifically designed to support individuals facing financial difficulties. Additionally, educational institutions, such as universities or training programs, may have clinics where supervised trainees offer counseling services at lower rates.

Directly discussing fees with mental health professionals can sometimes lead to negotiation, sliding scale agreements, or discounts for a specific number of sessions, even when such initiatives are not advertised. Creating a budget that prioritizes mental health treatment and identifies areas for potential cost-cutting is a practical step toward allocating funds for therapy.

Lastly, don't overlook community resources, such as local nonprofits or religious organizations, which may offer support or recommendations for affordable mental health services. Remember that prioritizing your mental health is crucial, and there are often resources available to help you access the care you need. Don't hesitate to reach out to professionals or organizations to discuss your situation and explore options for financial assistance.

Setting Realistic Goals

One of the main components of therapy is setting goals. Setting realistic goals in therapy is crucial for achieving positive outcomes and making meaningful progress. To begin this process, take time to reflect on your current situation and identify the specific challenges or issues you want to address during your therapeutic journey. This introspection allows you to pinpoint your emotional, behavioral, and relational needs.

Once you've identified your areas of focus, prioritize your goals based on their importance and their potential impact on your overall well-being. It's advisable to concentrate on a few key goals rather than attempting to address everything simultaneously.

When defining your goals, ensure clarity by expressing them in specific and concrete terms. Avoid vague or overly broad objectives, as specificity facilitates easier tracking of progress. Additionally, establish measurable criteria to evaluate your advancement. Measurable goals provide a tangible way to determine when a particular objective has been successfully achieved.

Breaking down larger goals into smaller, more manageable steps is a practical approach. This not only makes the process less overwhelming but also allows for a more effective tracking of your progress. Consider setting realistic timeframes for accomplishing your goals, understanding that personal growth and change take time. Some objectives may require more sessions to attain.

Collaborate closely with your therapist during this goal-setting process. Share your aspirations and concerns, and be open to their professional guidance in refining and shaping your objectives. Ensure that your goals align with your values and aspirations, as goals that resonate with your core values are more likely to motivate and drive positive change.

Frame your goals in terms of personal growth and development, emphasizing the journey towards improvement rather than solely focusing on the elimination of problems. This approach fosters a positive mindset and resilience, acknowledging that setbacks may occur.

Celebrate the progress you make along the way, recognizing and acknowledging small victories. This celebration not only boosts motivation but also reinforces the positive impact of therapy. Regularly review your goals with your therapist, assessing progress, discussing any changes in your circumstances, and adjusting goals as needed to ensure they remain relevant throughout your therapeutic experience.

Being Consistent With Treatment

Your mental health professional will want you to be consistent in your efforts. Consistency is paramount when undergoing treatment for phobias. Establishing a routine that incorporates therapy sessions, self-help strategies, and prescribed interventions is crucial for sustained progress. Begin by committing to regular therapy or psychiatry appointments and actively engaging in the therapeutic process. Consistency in attendance ensures that you receive the necessary support and guidance from your therapist, fostering a trusting and therapeutic relationship.

Beyond formal therapy sessions, it's essential to integrate therapeutic techniques into your daily life. Consistently practice exposure exercises, cognitive-behavioral strategies, or mindfulness techniques as recommended by your therapist. Repetition and regular application of these techniques contribute to desensitization and the gradual lessening of phobic responses.

Developing a consistent routine for facing and challenging your fears is key. Consistency in exposing yourself to the phobic stimuli, whether gradually or in planned intervals, helps build resilience and reduces the intensity of phobic reactions over time. This regular exposure is a fundamental aspect of many therapeutic approaches for phobias.

Adherence to any prescribed medications, if applicable, is another crucial element of consistency. Taking medications as directed by your healthcare provider ensures that the pharmacological aspect of treatment remains effective and contributes to overall therapeutic success. You never want to cease taking mental health meds without consulting your doctor because doing so can lead to extreme side effects that may worsen your mental or even physical health.

Additionally, maintaining open communication with your therapist about challenges, progress, and any adjustments needed in your treatment plan is vital. Consistency in sharing your experiences allows your therapist to tailor the approach to your evolving needs.

It's important to recognize that progress in overcoming phobias may take time, and setbacks may occur. Consistency in your commitment to treatment, even during challenging moments, is a testament to your dedication to personal growth. When you "fall off" and aren't consistent, don't give up. Instead, commit yourself to do better going forward. Celebrate small victories along the way and acknowledge the positive steps you take, reinforcing the importance of staying consistent in your therapeutic journey.

Being consistent with treatment for phobias involves a commitment to regular therapy sessions, the integration of therapeutic techniques into daily life, consistent exposure to phobic stimuli, adherence to prescribed medications, and ongoing communication with your therapist. This steadfast dedication lays the foundation for long-term success on the pathway to healing.

A Pathway to Healing

In the realm of conquering phobias, seeking professional and social help is not just an option; it is a strategic choice that aligns with the complexity of these challenges. Finding the right mental health professional requires a blend of intentionality, awareness, and a commitment to one's well-being. It also requires financial considerations. Professional help should be assisted by social support, which offers outlet and support beyond the hours of professional appointments. As individuals take this courageous step towards healing, they open doors to insights, coping strategies, and a therapeutic alliance that can illuminate the path towards lasting recovery. In the compassionate embrace of all types of support, the journey to conquer phobias becomes a collaborative and transformative one.

You are now equipped with a profound understanding of the building blocks for the journey ahead. A fortified support system, the discernment to seek professional help when needed, and the art of setting and celebrating realistic goals lay the groundwork for a transformative journey. The path to conquering phobias is not a solitary one, and with these tools, individuals can navigate the challenges with resilience, determination, and the unwavering belief in their capacity for liberation from phobias.

Chapter Four

Behavioral Techniques

When it comes to taking on your phobias, behavioral techniques stand as stalwart pillars, providing individuals with tangible tools to face their fears head-on. This chapter delves into some of the most common methods that are used to help people with crippling phobias—unveiling their transformative potential in the journey toward liberation from irrational anxieties.

Exposure Therapy: Unmasking the Fear, One Step at a Time

At the heart of behavioral techniques lies exposure therapy, a cornerstone in the treatment of phobias. This method is founded on the principle of systematically exposing individuals to the very objects or situations that trigger their fears. The belief is that, through repeated and controlled exposure, individuals can desensitize themselves to the feared stimuli, ultimately reducing their anxiety response.

What is Exposure Therapy?

Exposure therapy is a therapeutic technique used to treat various anxiety disorders, including phobias, post-traumatic stress disorder (PTSD), obsessive-compulsive disorder (OCD), and panic disorder. It involves systematically exposing individuals to the source of their fear or anxiety in a controlled and gradual manner.

The core principle of exposure therapy is based on the idea of habituation, which is the process of becoming desensitized to a feared stimulus through repeated and prolonged exposure. By confronting the feared object, situation, or thought in a safe environment, individuals learn that their feared outcomes are unlikely to occur or that they can cope with the anxiety they experience.

History of Exposure Therapy

Exposure therapy has a rich history marked by significant developments in understanding and treating anxiety disorders. Its roots can be traced back to the early 20th century when behavioral psychology began to gain prominence. The works of behaviorists such as John B. Watson and B.F. Skinner laid the groundwork for the principles that underpin exposure therapy today.

One of the earliest applications of exposure techniques can be found in Mary Cover Jones's pioneering work during the 1920s. Jones is often considered the "mother of behavior therapy" for her famous study on the desensitization of fear in children. Through systematic desensitization, she demonstrated that fears could be diminished by gradually exposing individuals to feared stimuli while they remained in a relaxed state. This set the stage for the development of exposure therapy as a systematic and evidence-based approach.

However, the formalization of exposure therapy as a distinct therapeutic technique gained momentum in the latter half of the 20th century. Joseph Wolpe, a South African psychiatrist, played a pivotal role in shaping exposure therapy with the introduction of systematic desensitization in the 1950s. Wolpe's method involved a step-by-step process of exposing individuals to anxiety-provoking stimuli while guiding them through relaxation exercises. This approach became a cornerstone in the treatment of various anxiety disorders.

The 1980s saw the emergence of cognitive-behavioral therapy (CBT), incorporating cognitive restructuring with behavioral techniques. Within this framework, exposure therapy gained further recognition and was integrated into comprehensive treatment protocols for conditions such as phobias, panic disorder, obsessive-compulsive disorder (OCD), and post-traumatic stress disorder (PTSD).

In recent decades, exposure therapy has continued to evolve with the incorporation of technology. Virtual reality exposure therapy (VRET) has been developed to simulate real-life situations in a controlled environment, providing a novel and effective way to expose individuals to feared stimuli. This innovation expands the applicability of exposure therapy, particularly in treating PTSD and specific phobias.

Throughout its history, exposure therapy has consistently demonstrated its effectiveness in helping individuals confront and overcome anxiety. Research findings and clinical success stories have contributed to its widespread acceptance as a key component of evidence-based treatments for anxiety-related disorders, showcasing its enduring significance in the field of mental health.

Types of Exposure Therapy

Exposure therapy can take different forms, including:

- In Vivo Exposure: Involves real-life exposure to the feared stimulus or situation. For example, someone with a fear of heights might gradually expose themselves to increasing heights, starting from standing on a chair and progressing to higher elevations over time.

- Imaginal Exposure: Involves exposure to the feared stimulus through imagination or visualization. This is often used for traumatic memories or situations that cannot be recreated in real life. Individuals are guided to vividly imagine the feared scenario in detail.

- Virtual Reality Exposure (VRE): Involves exposure to computer-generated simulations of the feared stimulus or situation. This method is particularly useful when real-life exposure is not feasible or safe. For example, individuals with a fear of flying can undergo exposure therapy using virtual reality simulations of airplane flights.

- Interoceptive Exposure: Involves exposure to bodily sensations associated with anxiety or panic attacks. This can include activities such as hyperventilating or spinning in a chair to induce physical sensations similar to those experienced during a panic attack.

The Heart of Exposure Therapy

Exposure therapy is typically conducted in a structured and gradual manner, starting with less anxiety-provoking stimuli and progressing to more challenging ones as individuals become more comfortable. It is often combined with other therapeutic techniques, such as cognitive restructuring and relaxation training, to maximize its effectiveness.

Control is crucial to ensuring the efficacy of exposures. The exposure is not haphazard, and acting too rashly in one's exposure can cause unwanted side effects; exposure must be a meticulously planned and controlled confrontation. This ensures that individuals navigate the process at a pace that suits their comfort level, fostering a sense of empowerment rather than overwhelm.

The types of techniques and exposures you will need depend on the exact nature of your phobia as well as any other co-occurring conditions you may have. For example, if you also have depression, you may have to treat depression first before you can start to work on exposures because you need to be in a suitable mindset to get through challenging exposures. However, there's no exact formula of how treatment needs to work because people all have different goals and desires when it comes to mental health care. That's why it's so useful to have a mental health professional who knows how to guide you through the process with care.

This process can take months or years to complete. Exposure therapy operates on the principle of repetition. This repetition serves as a catalyst for the brain to reevaluate the perceived threat, recalibrating its response over time, so you have to be patient with the process and be willing to not only commit a lot of emotional energy but also time.

The ultimate goal of exposure therapy is liberation—liberation from the shackles of irrational fears. As individuals expose themselves to feared stimuli, their anxiety response diminishes. Desensitization becomes the key that unlocks the chains, allowing individuals to approach once-dreaded objects or situations with newfound courage.

Guided Steps: Navigating Exposure with Purpose

From the identification of feared stimuli to the meticulous planning of exposures, each step is a deliberate stride toward freedom from phobias. While many people choose to embark on their exposure therapy journey with a therapist, it's possible to also take self-guided steps to emulate the process. You'll have to be more careful when working on your own, and it may take more time, but by confronting your fear, you can heal at a pace that fits your needs.

Understanding Fear

The first step to understanding fear involves a courageous dive into one's inner world. You can use introspection to probe the depths of your emotions and thoughts. What are the triggers that send ripples of anxiety through your body? Is it the dizzying heights that evoke a sense of vulnerability, the complexities of social situations that spark unease, or the enclosed spaces that suffocate with fear? This introspection is a voyage of self-discovery, where the roots of your anxiety are unearthed and you start to understand what is deeper than the fears. There are usually complex experiences and insecurities that build phobias.

Fear is not a monolithic entity; it wears myriad masks. Some things about your fear will be initially obvious while other things may only occur to you months or even years from now. With practice, you can learn to identify the specific stimuli that ignite their anxieties. Is it the sight of a spider, the prospect of speaking in public, or the sensation of being in an elevator? Each fear is unique, and its identification becomes the first crucial step towards understanding the intricacies of the phobia.

When you understand what fears you can have, you can name them, and identification is vital if you want to find answers for whatever your phobia is. As long as your phobia remains enigmatic, it still has the power to ruin your life and leave you feeling uncomfortable in your own skin.

Creating a Fear Hierarchy

Once the fears are identified, the next step involves creating a fear hierarchy—a structured list that ranks these fears from least to most anxiety-inducing. This hierarchy becomes the scaffolding upon which the exposure journey is constructed, ensuring a gradual and manageable progression. The fear hierarchy serves as more than just a list; it becomes a structured progression with a purpose, offering a scaffolding for exposure and building bridges to liberation. Each fear, thoughtfully ranked, becomes a steppingstone toward freedom from anxiety.

Follow these steps to create a fear hierarchy:

- List Your Fears: Begin by creating a comprehensive list of all the fears or phobias you want to address. Write them down, ensuring that you have a clear and exhaustive list.

- Assess Severity: Evaluate the severity of each fear. Consider how much distress or interference each fear causes in your daily life. Rank them from the most severe to the least severe.

- Consider Daily Impact: Reflect on how each fear affects your daily functioning. Take into account whether the fear limits your activities, relationships, or overall quality of life.

- Rate Emotional Distress: Assign a numerical rating to each fear based on the level of emotional distress it generates. You might use a scale, such as 1 to 10, with 10 being the most distressing. This provides a quantitative measure for comparison.

- Identify Avoidance Behaviors: Explore the avoidance behaviors associated with each fear. The more avoidance behaviors linked to a particular fear, the more impactful it may be on your life.

- Consider Long-Term Goals: Think about your long-term goals and which fears, if addressed, would have the most significant positive impact on your life. This could involve considering personal or professional aspirations.

- Consult with a Therapist: If you are working with a therapist, discuss your list with them. They can provide valuable insights, help you explore underlying patterns, and assist in developing a strategic plan for exposure therapy.

- Prioritize Gradual Exposure: If using exposure therapy, prioritize fears for gradual exposure. Start with the fear that is the least distressing and work your way up the hierarchy as you build confidence and tolerance.

- Review and Update Regularly: Periodically review and update your fear ranking. As you make progress in therapy, some fears may become less distressing or lose their significance. Adjust your ranking accordingly.

- Acknowledge Progress: Acknowledge and celebrate your achievements as you confront and overcome each fear. This positive reinforcement can motivate you to continue facing challenges.

Planning Exposures

The exposure plan is not a one-size-fits-all template; it is a bespoke creation tailored to the individual's fears, comfort level, and unique pace. Consideration for individual nuances is paramount as the plan takes shape, ensuring that each exposure is both challenging and manageable. Whether facing a fear of public speaking or confronting social anxieties, the exposure plan becomes a personalized roadmap guiding individuals toward triumph.

Planning exposures require you to be honest with yourself and to avoid making excuses about why you can't do something. You don't want to be overly harsh with yourself, but you also want to make sure that you are embarking on the journey with candor and patience.

Here is a step-by-step guide on how to plan exposures for phobias:

- Start with Lower-Level Exposures: Initiate exposure exercises with the least anxiety-provoking scenarios from your hierarchy. Gradually expose yourself to these situations while practicing relaxation techniques. This step-by-step approach allows for a controlled and manageable progression.

- Repeat and Reinforce: Repeat exposure exercises for each level of your hierarchy, gradually moving up as you become more comfortable. Repetition is crucial for desensitization and the reduction of anxiety responses. Reinforce positive experiences and achievements during exposures.

- Increase Difficulty Gradually: As you gain confidence and tolerance, incrementally increase the difficulty of exposures. Move to higher levels in your hierarchy, challenging yourself to face more anxiety-provoking situations. The key is to progress at a pace that feels manageable for you.

- Evaluate and Adjust: Regularly evaluate your progress with your therapist. Discuss the effectiveness of exposure exercises, any challenges faced, and adjustments needed to the plan. Flexibility is essential, and modifications to the exposure plan may be necessary based on your evolving needs and experiences.

- Celebrate Successes and Use Constructive Criticism: Acknowledge and celebrate your successes after each exposure. Recognize the progress you've made and the courage it took to face your fears. Also think about things you could have done better, which will help you shape future exposure.

- Integrate Exposures into Daily Life: Extend exposure exercises into your daily life whenever possible. Practice facing feared situations outside of therapy to enhance generalization and long-term effectiveness.

Remember, exposure therapy is most effective when approached systematically, with patience and persistence. Working collaboratively with a therapist ensures that exposures are tailored to your specific needs and that you have the necessary support throughout the process.

Chapter Five

Taking Charge of the Journey

In exposure therapy, empowerment takes center stage. Exposure therapy is not a passive experience but a dynamic collaboration—an alliance between the individual and the therapeutic process. Through the provision of a roadmap for gradual exposure, this therapeutic journey unfolds as a partnership, cultivating a profound sense of control over fears that once seemed insurmountable.

Fostering Control Over Uncontrollable Fears

Empowerment in exposure therapy is synonymous with a sense of agency—an understanding that individuals have the power to influence their responses to feared stimuli. The exposure journey becomes a testament to this agency, challenging the notion that fears are uncontrollable. Each intentional exposure is a declaration of autonomy, eroding the grip of anxiety and replacing it with a newfound sense of mastery.

As individuals actively engage with the exposure process, the transformative impact is profound. What once felt overwhelming becomes manageable, and what seemed insurmountable becomes a conquered terrain. The therapeutic journey becomes a narrative of personal triumph, where the individual emerges not as a victim of fears but as a victor over them.

A Partnership Between Individual and Process

Exposure therapy transcends the conventional therapist-patient dynamic. It is a collaboration where the individual is not a passive recipient of treatment but an active participant in the journey. The exposure plan is a shared creation, evolving through dialogue and feedback. This collaboration instills a sense of ownership, making the therapy or self-guided journey a shared endeavor toward conquering fears.

During exposure sessions, individuals are not passive observers but active participants in the process. Whether facing a fear head-on or gradually exposing themselves, they play a pivotal role in all exposures. This active engagement cultivates resilience, reinforcing the understanding that they are not at the mercy of their fears but in command of their responses.

Building Resilience

Phobias can cast shadows over one's life, but within the shadows, the light of resilience can emerge as a guiding force. This chapter explores the profound journey of building resilience for individuals grappling with phobias. It unveils strategies, perspectives, and practices that empower them to navigate the challenges of exposure therapy and embrace a life liberated from the constraints of irrational fears.

Resilience is more than a buzzword; it's the essence of inner strength in the face of adversity. For individuals with phobias, building resilience involves cultivating the capacity to bounce back from setbacks, face fears with courage, and adapt to the challenges of exposure therapy. It is the foundation upon which the journey toward conquering phobias is built.

Resilience begins with a shift in perspective. Individuals are encouraged to view challenges not as insurmountable obstacles but as opportunities for growth. Phobias, once perceived as formidable foes, become stepping stones toward personal development. This shift in mindset lays the groundwork for the resilience-building journey. Individuals are guided to embrace small victories, gradually increasing the difficulty of exposures. Each conquered fear becomes a testament to their growing resilience, fostering a sense of accomplishment and fortitude.

Building resilience involves arming oneself with coping mechanisms. Techniques such as deep breathing, mindfulness, and positive self-talk become tools for navigating the emotional turbulence that exposure therapy may bring. These coping mechanisms serve as beacons, illuminating the path through the shadows of anxiety.

Mindset and Self-Compassion: Pillars of Resilience

A growth mindset is a cornerstone of improving your phobia. Individuals are encouraged to view challenges not as fixed limitations but as opportunities for learning and growth. Mistakes are reframed as stepping-stones toward mastery, fostering a mindset that bolsters resilience in the face of setbacks.

Individuals are guided to treat themselves with the same kindness they would offer a friend facing similar challenges. Embracing imperfections and setbacks with self-compassion becomes a soothing aid on the journey to overcoming phobias.

Reflection and Celebration: Milestones of Resilience

Recovery is a journey, not a destination. Regular reflection on progress becomes a reflective mirror, showcasing the distance traveled. Individuals are guided to recognize and celebrate even the smallest milestones, reinforcing the belief in their ability to face and conquer fears.

Celebrations are not reserved for grand achievements alone. Small victories, whether in exposure sessions or daily life, are celebrated. This intentional acknowledgment becomes a powerful motivator, fueling the resilience needed for the challenges that lie ahead.

Fostering Autonomy

Exposure therapy is designed with a structured approach, offering a clear path for facing fears systematically. The structured boundaries serve as a guide, providing a roadmap for individuals to follow. Within this framework, autonomy is not a departure from structure but an integration—a weaving of personal choices within the fabric of the therapeutic plan.

Autonomy involves making informed choices at each juncture. Individuals are encouraged to actively participate in decision-making, choosing exposure techniques, setting the pace, and determining the level of challenge. Informed choices become a compass, allowing individuals to navigate their fears in alignment with their comfort and progress.

Autonomy transforms the process from a standardized process into a deeply personal journey. Each exposure session becomes a reflection of individual choices, preferences, and readiness. The therapeutic journey is not imposed but chosen, fostering a sense of ownership that is essential for meaningful progress.

The empowerment derived from autonomy extends to the decision-making process. Individuals are not passive recipients of exposure techniques but active decision-makers, choosing what resonates with them. This empowerment becomes a catalyst for engagement, commitment, and resilience in the face of fears.

Autonomy extends to the personalization of exposure techniques. While the structured approach provides a repertoire of methods, individuals are empowered to choose techniques that align with their comfort levels. Whether it's systematic desensitization, in vivo exposure, or virtual reality, autonomy ensures that the chosen techniques resonate with the individual's preferences and readiness.

Autonomy allows for the flexible application of exposure techniques. Individuals can adapt and modify techniques based on their responses and evolving comfort levels. This flexibility ensures that the exposure process remains dynamic, responsive, and aligned with the individual's unique journey.

Stories of Triumph: Illuminating the Path Forward

These stories illustrate the transformative power of systematic exposure and the positive impact it can have on individuals' lives. These stories do not include all the phobias and treatment processes that exist, but they do illuminate how you can have a path forward to being a more healthy and well-balanced self.

Fear of Flying

Sarah had a debilitating fear of flying that prevented her from enjoying vacations or visiting family abroad. Through exposure therapy, she gradually exposed herself to elements associated with flying, such as watching videos of flights, visiting airports, and eventually taking short flights. Over time, her anxiety diminished, and she regained the freedom to explore the world without the burden of fear. She was thrilled when she was able to attend her cousin's destination wedding in Hawaii, something she could have never imagined doing at the start of therapy.

Social Anxiety

David struggled with social anxiety, making it challenging for him to engage in everyday social interactions. He avoided work functions whenever possible and rarely did anything with his friends. Exposure therapy guided him through a series of controlled exposures, starting with small group settings and progressively moving to larger gatherings. As he faced his fears, David developed confidence, built meaningful connections, and eventually conquered his social anxieties. He now has drinks with his coworkers after work and is closer than ever with his friends.

Claustrophobia

Mark faced severe claustrophobia, which hindered his ability to use elevators or navigate crowded spaces. Because of his fears, he felt limited in the activities he could do. Exposure therapy exposed him to enclosed spaces in a gradual and controlled manner. Beginning with short durations, he eventually worked his way up to longer periods, and he could ride elevators and move through crowded areas without the overwhelming anxiety that once paralyzed him. He went to a huge musical festival after years at not being able to go to concerts despite his love of music.

Public Speaking Phobia

Emily, an executive, struggled with a fear of public speaking that hindered her professional growth. Every performance review said she needed to speak up more. Exposure therapy involved progressively challenging her fear, starting with small presentations in front of supportive colleagues and gradually moving to larger audiences. Through this process, Emily not only overcame her fear but also excelled in her professional presentations. She actually grew to love making presentations. She still gets a little nervous, but she learned coping skills to deal with her nerves.

Arachnophobia

Jake had an intense fear of spiders (arachnophobia) that affected his daily life. Exposure therapy involved gradually introducing him to images of spiders, followed by observing videos and eventually interacting with spiders in a controlled environment. As Jake faced his fear, he realized that the perceived threat was exaggerated, leading to a significant reduction in anxiety. Before, Jake barely went outside because a spider could appear at anytime. He eventually began biking and found a great appreciation for the outdoors.

Fear of Heights

Alex had a deep-seated fear of heights that limited his ability to enjoy outdoor activities that his friends all loved. Exposure therapy exposed him to increasing heights, starting with low elevations and progressively moving to higher ones. Over time, Alex not only conquered his fear but also found joy in activities like hiking and rock climbing that were once unthinkable.

Writing Your Own Story

These stories demonstrate that exposure therapy can be a transformative and effective approach for overcoming various phobias. The key is the gradual and systematic exposure to feared stimuli, allowing individuals to reevaluate and recalibrate their responses, ultimately leading to liberation from irrational fears. You get to write the path the rest of your story will take because while phobias can make you feel powerless, you have plenty of choice in what how you respond to your fears.

Exposure therapy is a courageous unveiling—a shedding of the layers of fear to reveal the resilience within. The road ahead is paved with challenges, but it is also illuminated by the potential for profound transformation. As individuals unmask their fears, one step at a time, they embark on a journey toward liberation, courageously reclaiming control over their lives.

Chapter Six

Cognitive Strategies

As we embark on the next phase of our journey toward conquering phobias, Chapter 4 places the spotlight on how the way you think defines how you act. Cognitive strategies become our compass, guiding us through distorted thoughts and paving the way for a transformative shift in perspective. Through an exploration of cognitive distortions, cognitive restructuring exercises, and the cultivation of positive thinking, readers will discover the profound impact that harnessing the power of the mind can have on phobia recovery.

What Does Cognitive Mean?

"Cognitive" refers to mental processes and activities related to acquiring, processing, storing, and using information. It encompasses a wide range of mental functions, including perception, attention, memory, language, problem-solving, decision-making, and reasoning. Essentially, cognition involves the way individuals perceive, understand, and interact with the world around them.

In the realm of psychology, cognitive processes are central to various theoretical frameworks and therapeutic approaches. Cognitive psychology, for example, focuses on studying mental processes to understand how individuals think, learn, and remember information. Cognitive neuroscience explores the neural mechanisms underlying cognitive functions, providing insights into the biological basis of cognition.

The term "cognitive" is often associated with conscious mental activities, highlighting the role of awareness and intentional thought processes. Cognitive abilities are fundamental to human intelligence and play a crucial role in shaping behavior, emotions, and overall mental functioning.

In everyday language, when someone mentions cognitive skills or cognitive functioning, they are referring to the abilities related to thinking, learning, and problem-solving. These skills are essential for tasks such as reading, reasoning, planning, and adapting to new situations.

What are Cognitive Strategies?

Cognitive strategies refer to mental processes and techniques individuals use to acquire, process, organize, and apply information. These strategies involve conscious and intentional efforts to manage thoughts, perceptions, and problem-solving. Cognitive strategies are often employed to enhance learning, memory, and problem-solving skills, and they play a crucial role in various aspects of cognitive functioning.

In the context of psychology and mental health, cognitive strategies are frequently associated with approaches such as cognitive-behavioral therapy (CBT). In CBT, these strategies involve identifying and modifying distorted thought patterns and beliefs that contribute to emotional distress and maladaptive behaviors. Cognitive restructuring, thought challenging, and reframing are examples of cognitive strategies used to address irrational or negative thinking.

In educational settings, cognitive strategies are techniques students use to improve their learning and academic performance. These may include methods for organizing information, mnemonic devices for memory enhancement, and problem-solving approaches. These strategies are designed to optimize cognitive processes and facilitate more effective learning and information retention.

Cognitive strategies are versatile tools applied in various contexts to enhance cognitive functioning, promote effective decision-making, and manage thoughts and emotions. They encompass a range of mental processes, from basic attention and memory strategies to higher-order cognitive skills involved in critical thinking and problem-solving. The specific cognitive strategies employed can vary depending on the task, goal, or context in which they are applied. Thus, cognitive strategies will not only help you conquer your phobia, but they will also help you improve all parts of your life.

Understanding Cognitive Distortions: The Culprits Behind Irrational Fears

Cognitive distortions are systematic errors in thinking that individuals may engage in when interpreting events or situations. Coined by Aaron T. Beck, a pioneer in cognitive therapy, these distortions represent thought patterns that deviate from objective reality. They often involve biased and irrational interpretations of oneself, others, and the world, leading to negative emotions and behaviors.

There are several common types of cognitive distortions that individuals may exhibit. These include, but are not limited to, black-and-white thinking (seeing situations as all good or all bad), catastrophizing (expecting the worst possible outcome), overgeneralization (making broad negative conclusions based on limited evidence), and personalization (attributing external events to oneself without sufficient evidence).

Cognitive distortions can significantly impact mental health by contributing to feelings of anxiety, depression, and stress. When individuals consistently engage in distorted thinking patterns, it can reinforce negative beliefs about themselves, others, and the world. Over time, this negativity can perpetuate a cycle of maladaptive thoughts and emotions.

Cognitive distortions often manifest as automatic negative thoughts (ANTs), which are spontaneous and unhelpful thoughts that arise in response to situations. These thoughts are characterized by their speed and lack of conscious control, making them challenging to identify and challenge. CBT aims to help individuals recognize and modify these automatic negative thoughts.

In cognitive-behavioral therapy, the process of challenging and restructuring cognitive distortions is central to promoting emotional well-being. This involves actively questioning the validity and accuracy of distorted thoughts, considering alternative perspectives, and replacing irrational thoughts with more balanced and realistic ones. By challenging cognitive distortions, individuals can break free from negative thinking patterns and develop healthier ways of interpreting their experiences. This process is vital in phobias, which often perpetrate unhealthy thinking that makes sufferers feel fearful even when that fear is warranted.

Therapists often use various techniques to address cognitive distortions. These may include keeping thought records, where individuals document and analyze their thoughts, conducting behavioral experiments to test the validity of distorted beliefs, and learning mindfulness and relaxation techniques to increase awareness and manage distressing thoughts.

Addressing cognitive distortions not only improves immediate emotional well-being but also has long-term benefits. By cultivating awareness of thought patterns and developing skills to challenge distortions, individuals can build resilience, enhance problem-solving abilities, and foster a more positive and adaptive mindset. This process contributes to lasting improvements in phobia recovery and overall life satisfaction.

Recognizing and Challenging Distorted Thoughts: A Guided Journey

Armed with the understanding that cognitive distortions can be the invisible puppeteers of irrational fears, it's time for self-reflection. This section provides exercises designed to illuminate the common cognitive distortions associated with phobias. Through a series of reflective prompts and thought-provoking activities, readers gain the ability to identify the subtle distortions at play in their own thought processes.

Identification of Distorted Thoughts

The first step in challenging cognitive distortions during phobia recovery involves identifying and recognizing distorted thoughts related to the specific fear or phobia. Pay close attention to automatic negative thoughts (ANTs) that arise in response to the phobic stimuli or situations. These thoughts often contribute to heightened anxiety and reinforce the phobia.

Record and Analyze Thoughts

Keep a thought record or journal to document these automatic negative thoughts. Write down the specific thoughts that accompany the experience of the phobia. Include details about the situation, your emotional reactions, and any behavioral responses. This record becomes a valuable tool for later analysis and intervention.

Question the Validity of Thoughts

Once thoughts are documented, systematically question their validity. Ask yourself whether the thoughts are based on evidence, whether they are extreme or exaggerated, and whether there are alternative, more balanced interpretations. Challenge the automatic negative thoughts by considering whether they align with objective reality or if they are distorted perceptions.

Explore Evidence Supporting and Opposing Thoughts

Engage in a process of evidence-based exploration. Identify evidence that supports the distorted thoughts and evidence that contradicts them. This objective analysis helps individuals gain a more balanced perspective on the phobic stimuli and challenge the irrational beliefs that contribute to the fear.

Consider Alternative Interpretations

Encourage yourself to consider alternative interpretations of the phobic stimuli or situations. This involves exploring more realistic and less catastrophic explanations for what might happen. By generating alternative thoughts, you open the door to viewing the phobia from a less threatening and more manageable perspective.

Cognitive Restructuring Techniques

Practice cognitive restructuring techniques, which involve consciously replacing distorted thoughts with more balanced and adaptive ones. This may include creating positive affirmations or reframing negative statements into more constructive language. Regularly reinforce these new thought patterns to build a more positive and resilient mindset.

Behavioral Experiments

Conduct behavioral experiments to test the validity of distorted thoughts. Gradually expose yourself to the phobic stimuli in a controlled and systematic way, noting the actual outcomes versus the anticipated negative consequences. This process helps challenge irrational beliefs and provides real-world evidence to counter distorted thoughts.

The Mind-Body Connection: Nurturing Mental Well-Being

The mind-body connection is explored as a vital aspect of cognitive strategies. Recognizing how thoughts and emotions influence physical well-being, readers are encouraged to embrace holistic practices that contribute to mental and emotional equilibrium.

Recognizing the Influence: Thoughts as Architects of Well-Being

When confronted with phobias, the body often responds with heightened stress levels, manifesting in tension, increased heart rate, and other physical reactions. Understanding this mind-body link becomes a foundational step in the journey toward holistic well-being.

The mind-body connection refers to the intricate and bidirectional relationship between the mind (mental processes, thoughts, and emotions) and the body (physical health, sensations, and behaviors). This concept acknowledges that mental and emotional states can significantly influence physical well-being, and conversely, physical health can impact mental and emotional states. The interconnectedness of the mind and body is a fundamental aspect of holistic health and has profound implications for overall well-being, particularly in the treatment of phobias.

At its core, the mind-body connection recognizes that mental and emotional factors can influence physical health outcomes. For example, chronic stress, anxiety, or depression can contribute to the development or exacerbation of physical conditions such as cardiovascular disease, gastrointestinal issues, or immune system dysfunction. The release of stress hormones like cortisol and adrenaline during prolonged periods of stress can have measurable effects on various bodily functions.

Conversely, physical health can impact mental and emotional well-being. Ailments, chronic pain, or physical discomfort can contribute to mood disorders, fatigue, and changes in cognitive function. The experience of physical pain can lead to emotional distress, impacting mental states and affecting one's overall quality of life. Physical stimuli can lead to development of phobias as a protective response.

The mind-body connection is supported by scientific evidence demonstrating the impact of psychological interventions on physical health outcomes. Practices such as mindfulness meditation, relaxation techniques, and cognitive-behavioral therapy have been shown to positively influence both mental and physical health. These interventions can reduce stress, improve mood, and contribute to better physiological functioning. Thus, they an work on how your mind and body are linked rather than just confronting the roots of your disorder.

Additionally, the mind-body connection plays a crucial role in the placebo effect, where the belief in the effectiveness of a treatment can lead to real physiological changes. The power of positive thinking and belief in recovery can influence outcomes, highlighting the intricate interplay between mental states and physical responses. Accordingly, if you think you can't recover, you won't, but if you think you can recover, recovery is more likely.

Establishing a Mind-Body Connection

You can take steps to promote a healthy mind-body connection. Many of these steps are simple, so they don't require a lot of effort to get a lot of results.

Conscious control of the breath is a powerful tool for establishing a mind-body connection. Engaging in deep diaphragmatic breathing and relaxation techniques can activate the body's relaxation response, reducing stress and promoting a sense of calm. By intentionally directing the breath, individuals can influence physiological responses and bring awareness to the present moment, fostering a more harmonious connection between the mind and body.

You can also engage in exercises that heighten body awareness. Progressive muscle relaxation, where you systematically tense and release different muscle groups, can help release physical tension and increase awareness of bodily sensations. Similarly, body scan exercises involve mentally scanning each part of the body, promoting a deeper connection to bodily sensations and facilitating relaxation.

You can try activities that encourage a sense of embodiment, such as dance, hiking, or any form of physical exercise that brings joy. These activities not only contribute to physical health but also provide an opportunity to be fully present in the body. Moving with awareness allows individuals to appreciate the connection between physical sensations and emotional states.

As is a trend throughout this book, regular self-reflection and journaling can deepen the understanding of the mind-body connection. Take time to explore and express thoughts, emotions, and physical sensations. Journaling provides a platform to track patterns, identify triggers, and observe the interplay between mental and physical states, fostering greater self-awareness.

Creating a mind-body connection involves incorporating intentional practices that promote awareness, mindfulness, and a holistic view of well-being. Whether through movement, breathwork, or self-reflection, these practices foster a deeper understanding of the interconnectedness between mental and physical states, contributing to a more balanced and harmonious life.

Embracing the Journey: A New Mental Landscape

As you engage with the cognitive strategies presented in this chapter, may you discover the transformative potential residing within your own thoughts. May the exercises and practices become stepping-stones toward a mental landscape where courage, resilience, and positive thinking reign supreme. The journey toward conquering phobias is not only one of external confrontations but a profound exploration of the inner realms of the mind, and with each shift in perspective, you draw closer to the freedom you seek.

Chapter Seven

Coping Mechanisms and Techniques

The journey through life is fraught with challenges, and in the face of adversity, individuals often turn to coping mechanisms and techniques as their compass for navigating the storms of stress, uncertainty, and emotional turmoil. Coping mechanisms represent the intricate web of psychological strategies and behaviors that individuals employ to adapt, endure, and even thrive in the face of life's complexities. These mechanisms serve as the threads that weave through the fabric of emotional resilience, offering pathways to manage stressors, process emotions, and foster overall well-being.

What Does it Mean to Cope?

To cope means to effectively deal with, manage, or adapt to challenges, stressors, difficulties, or changes in life. Coping involves utilizing various strategies, resources, and skills to navigate and overcome situations that may be emotionally, mentally, or physically demanding.

Effective coping does not necessarily mean eliminating stressors but rather finding constructive ways to manage and mitigate their impact on one's well-being. Ultimately, coping is a fundamental aspect of resilience and personal growth, allowing individuals to navigate life's ups and downs with greater adaptability and emotional stability.

What Are Coping Mechanisms?

Coping mechanisms refer to adaptive strategies and behaviors that individuals employ to manage and navigate the challenges presented by stress, adversity, or emotional distress. These mechanisms serve as psychological tools to help individuals cope with various situations, maintain emotional well-being, and navigate the complexities of life. Coping mechanisms can be both adaptive and maladaptive, depending on their effectiveness in promoting well-being and maintaining psychological stability. Coping mechanisms can be conscious or unconscious, and they play a crucial role in promoting resilience, reducing anxiety, and fostering overall mental health.

At their core, coping mechanisms are mechanisms of psychological adaptation. When individuals encounter stressors, whether they be external events, internal conflicts, or emotional triggers, coping mechanisms come into play to help mitigate the impact of these stressors on mental and emotional well-being. The goal of coping mechanisms is not only to endure or survive challenging circumstances but also to facilitate effective problem-solving, emotional regulation, and personal growth.

Coping mechanisms can manifest in various forms, ranging from cognitive strategies that involve altering thought patterns to behavioral techniques that influence actions and reactions. Additionally, coping mechanisms may be categorized as either adaptive or maladaptive. Adaptive coping mechanisms are those that contribute positively to an individual's well-being, fostering resilience and effective stress management. In contrast, maladaptive coping mechanisms may provide temporary relief but can ultimately be detrimental to mental health, inhibiting long-term growth and well-being.

Common examples of coping mechanisms include seeking social support, engaging in relaxation techniques, practicing mindfulness, utilizing problem-solving skills, and seeking professional help when needed. The effectiveness of coping mechanisms can vary from person to person, and individuals often develop a repertoire of strategies that suit their unique personalities, circumstances, and coping styles.

It's important to note that coping mechanisms are dynamic and can evolve over time as individuals face new challenges and experiences. Furthermore, cultivating a diverse set of coping mechanisms contributes to a more comprehensive and adaptable approach to managing life's inevitable stressors. Overall, understanding and developing effective coping mechanisms are integral components of maintaining mental and emotional well-being in the face of life's complexities.

How Coping Mechanisms Help Phobias?

Coping mechanisms play a pivotal role in managing and alleviating phobias. When confronted with irrational fears that can be debilitating, coping mechanisms act as invaluable tools that individuals can harness to regain a sense of control and stability. These adaptive strategies serve as a bridge between the overwhelming anxiety triggered by phobic stimuli and the desire for a more composed and measured response.

One of the primary ways coping mechanisms aid in phobia management is by offering a structured approach to confront and navigate feared situations. Exposure therapy involves gradually facing and acclimating oneself to the source of fear, ultimately leading to desensitization. This deliberate and controlled exposure empowers individuals to rewrite their emotional responses, fostering resilience in the face of phobic triggers.

Cognitive coping mechanisms also play a crucial role by addressing distorted thought patterns associated with phobias. Techniques such as cognitive restructuring encourage individuals to recognize and challenge irrational beliefs, replacing them with more realistic and balanced perspectives. This process disrupts the cognitive distortions that contribute to the amplification of phobic fears.

Additionally, relaxation techniques serve as coping mechanisms that can help manage the physical manifestations of anxiety associated with phobias. Deep breathing, progressive muscle relaxation, and mindfulness exercises contribute to a calmer physiological state, diminishing the intensity of fear responses.

Moreover, coping mechanisms empower individuals to navigate setbacks and relapses in the journey to conquer phobias. By providing tools for emotional regulation and resilience, these strategies become a lifeline during challenging moments, preventing individuals from feeling overwhelmed or defeated.

In essence, coping mechanisms offer a multifaceted toolkit for individuals grappling with phobias, providing them with the means to confront fears, reframe thought patterns, and cultivate a resilient mindset. As indispensable companions on the journey to overcoming irrational fears, coping mechanisms become pillars of support, helping individuals rebuild their lives with newfound strength and courage.

The Difference Between Good and Bad Coping Mechanisms

As we've briefly discussed, coping mechanisms, can be categorized into good and bad coping mechanisms based on their effectiveness and long-term impact. Understanding this distinction is crucial for fostering mental well-being and effective recovery.

Good coping mechanisms are those that contribute to adaptive, positive, and sustainable responses to stressors. These strategies promote emotional regulation, resilience, and overall well-being. Examples of good coping mechanisms include seeking social support, engaging in regular physical exercise, practicing mindfulness, maintaining a healthy lifestyle, and utilizing problem-solving skills. These approaches help individuals address the root causes of stress, build emotional strength, and develop a positive outlook on challenges.

On the other hand, bad coping mechanisms, often referred to as maladaptive or unhealthy strategies, provide temporary relief but may lead to negative consequences in the long run. Examples of bad coping mechanisms include substance abuse, excessive alcohol consumption, avoidance, denial, procrastination, and unhealthy eating habits. While these tactics might offer short-term escape or distraction, they do not address the underlying issues and may contribute to increased stress, impaired mental health, and a cycle of dependency.

The key difference lies in the sustainability and impact on overall well-being. Good coping mechanisms empower individuals to confront challenges, adapt to stressors, and maintain a healthy mental state. They contribute to personal growth and resilience over time. In contrast, bad coping mechanisms offer momentary relief but often result in increased stress, exacerbation of problems, and potential harm to mental and physical health.

Recognizing the difference between good and bad coping mechanisms allows individuals to make informed choices when facing challenges. Building a repertoire of effective coping strategies enhances one's ability to navigate life's ups and downs, fostering long-term mental and emotional well-being.

How to Instill Healthy Coping Mechanisms

Instilling healthy coping mechanisms is a proactive and empowering process that involves intentional efforts to cultivate positive habits. One effective approach is self-awareness, which involves recognizing and understanding one's emotions, triggers, and stressors. By developing a keen awareness of emotional responses, individuals can pinpoint areas that may require healthier coping mechanisms and tailor their strategies accordingly.

Building a strong support network is a key component of instilling healthy coping mechanisms. Surrounding oneself with understanding and empathetic friends, family, or support groups creates a foundation for emotional support. Sharing thoughts and feelings with trusted individuals fosters a sense of connection and provides opportunities for receiving valuable feedback and guidance.

Education plays a vital role in instilling healthy coping mechanisms. Learning about various coping strategies, stress management techniques, and the importance of self-care empowers individuals to make informed choices. Educational resources, workshops, or therapy sessions can provide valuable insights and equip individuals with the knowledge needed to select and implement effective coping mechanisms.

Setting realistic goals is a crucial aspect of instilling healthy coping mechanisms. Individuals can start by identifying specific areas they want to improve or certain stressors they want to manage better. Establishing achievable and measurable goals ensures that the process of cultivating healthy coping habits is gradual and sustainable, contributing to long-term success.

Practicing mindfulness is another essential component. Mindfulness involves staying present in the current moment without judgment. Techniques such as meditation, deep breathing, or guided imagery can help individuals manage stress, reduce anxiety, and instill a sense of calm. Consistent practice of mindfulness contributes to the development of healthier coping mechanisms over time.

Consistency and perseverance are key elements in the process of instilling healthy coping mechanisms. Developing new habits takes time, and individuals should be patient with themselves as they work towards adopting healthier approaches to stress and challenges. Celebrating small victories along the way reinforces positive behavior and motivates continued efforts.

Ultimately, instilling healthy coping mechanisms is a holistic journey that involves self-reflection, education, support, goal-setting, mindfulness, and persistence. By actively engaging in this process, individuals can transform their approach to stress, build resilience, and promote overall mental well-being.

Examples of Good Coping Mechanisms

There are many ways that you can cope in a healthy way. The methods you choose to employ will depend on what makes you feel safe and secure as well as your lifestyle. Not all coping mechanisms will work for everyone, and that's okay.

Practicing Mindfulness

Another effective coping mechanism is practicing mindfulness. Mindfulness involves being present in the moment without judgment, allowing individuals to manage stress by focusing on the current experience. Techniques such as deep breathing, meditation, or yoga promote relaxation, reduce anxiety, and enhance overall emotional well-being. Incorporating mindfulness into daily routines provides individuals with a powerful tool for managing stressors.

Practicing mindfulness involves cultivating a heightened awareness and presence in the current moment, without judgment. Use the following tips to be more mindful:

- Schedule dedicated time for formal mindfulness practice, such as meditation. Start with short sessions, gradually increasing the duration as you become more comfortable. Use guided meditation apps or videos if you're new to meditation.

- Begin by paying attention to your breath. Focus on the sensation of breathing in and out. You can do this anywhere, at any time. Notice the rise and fall of your chest or the sensation of the breath passing through your nostrils.

- Choose an object, such as a flower, and observe it mindfully. Notice its colors, textures, and any subtle details. Allow yourself to fully engage with the sensory experience without getting lost in thoughts or judgments.

- Lie down or sit comfortably and bring attention to different parts of your body, starting from your toes and moving up to your head. Notice any sensations, tension, or areas of comfort. This practice enhances bodily awareness and relaxation.

- While walking, pay attention to each step and the sensations in your feet. Feel the ground beneath you, notice the movement of your body, and observe your surroundings. Walking mindfully brings awareness to a daily activity.

- Incorporate mindful breathing into your daily routine. Take a few mindful breaths before starting a task, during breaks, or when you find yourself feeling stressed. This helps anchor you to the present moment.

- Practice mindful eating by paying attention to each bite. Notice the flavors, textures, and smells of your food. Eat slowly and savor each moment. This practice fosters a deeper connection with the act of eating.

- Engage fully in whatever you're doing. Whether it's washing dishes, reading a book, or having a conversation, bring your full attention to the activity. Resist the urge to multitask or let your mind wander.

- Cultivate an attitude of non-judgmental awareness. When thoughts arise, observe them without attaching labels of good or bad. Allow thoughts to come and go, returning your focus to the present moment.

- Utilize mindfulness apps like Headspace, Calm, or Insight Timer. These platforms offer guided meditations, mindfulness exercises, and resources to support your practice.

- Consider joining a mindfulness group or taking a class. Group settings can provide support, motivation, and a sense of community in your mindfulness journey.

- Mindfulness is a skill that develops over time. Be patient and compassionate with yourself as you embark on this journey. It's normal for your mind to wander; gently bring your attention back to the present when it does.

Mindfulness is about being present without judgment. Consistent practice can lead to increased awareness, reduced stress, and an enhanced sense of well-being over time.

Exercise

Regular physical exercise is a fundamental coping mechanism that contributes to both mental and physical well-being. Exercise releases endorphins, the body's natural mood lifters, and helps reduce stress hormones. Whether it's a brisk walk, a workout session, or participating in a favorite sport, physical activity has positive effects on mood, cognitive function, and overall mental health.

- Incorporating more exercise into your routine is a fantastic goal for physical and mental well-being. Here are some tips to help you get more exercise:

- Start with achievable goals. Whether it's a daily walk or a weekly workout session, setting realistic targets helps build consistency.

- Choose exercises or activities that you genuinely enjoy. This could be anything from dancing and hiking to playing a sport. When it's enjoyable, it's more likely to become a regular part of your routine.

- Variety keeps things interesting. Try different types of exercises to prevent boredom and target various muscle groups. This could include cardio, strength training, yoga, or team sports.

- Exercise with friends or join group classes. Having a social component can make exercise more fun and provide built-in accountability.

- Treat exercise like any other important appointment. Schedule it into your calendar and prioritize it as you would any other commitment.

- Look for opportunities to be active throughout the day. Take the stairs instead of the elevator, walk or bike to work, or incorporate quick exercises during breaks.

- Fitness apps and trackers can help you set goals, monitor your progress, and provide motivation. Many of them offer personalized workout plans and reminders.

- If you're new to exercise or restarting after a break, start with shorter sessions. Gradually increase the duration and intensity to avoid burnout or injury.

- Set reminders on your phone or computer to prompt you to get up and move. These nudges can be helpful, especially if you have a sedentary job.

- Develop a space at home dedicated to exercise. It could be a corner with a yoga mat and some weights. Having a designated area makes it easier to incorporate quick workouts into your day.

- Establish a system of rewards for achieving your exercise goals. Treat yourself to something special after completing a certain number of workouts or reaching a fitness milestone.

- Life is unpredictable, and schedules may change. Be flexible in adjusting your workout routine to accommodate unexpected events without feeling discouraged.

- Morning workouts can energize you for the day and eliminate the risk of scheduling conflicts later on. Establishing a morning exercise routine can create consistency.

- Consider hiring a personal trainer or joining a fitness class. Professional guidance can provide structure, motivation, and ensure you're performing exercises correctly.

Remember, the key is to find activities that you enjoy and that fit into your lifestyle. Consistency is more important than intensity, so gradually build up to more challenging workouts over time. Listen to your body, stay motivated, and make exercise a sustainable and enjoyable part of your daily routine.

Good Sleep

Adequate and quality sleep plays a crucial role in phobia recovery by contributing to emotional regulation, cognitive functioning, and overall mental well-being. Sleep serves as a foundational pillar for the consolidation of new learning and the processing of emotional experiences, both of which are essential components of cognitive-behavioral therapies used in phobia treatment.

When individuals with phobias experience consistent, restorative sleep, they are better equipped to manage anxiety, process exposure therapy sessions, and engage more effectively in cognitive restructuring. Additionally, sufficient sleep supports the regulation of stress hormones, fostering emotional resilience and reducing the likelihood of heightened anxiety, which is often associated with phobias. Prioritizing healthy sleep habits becomes integral to optimizing the effectiveness of therapeutic interventions and promoting a comprehensive approach to phobia recovery.

Ensuring a good night's sleep is crucial for overall health and well-being. Thus, you cannot recover from a phobia without sleep. Here are several ways to promote better sleep:

- Maintain a regular sleep schedule by going to bed and waking up at the same time every day, even on weekends. This helps regulate your body's internal clock and promotes a more consistent sleep pattern.

- Establish calming bedtime rituals to signal to your body that it's time to wind down. This could include activities like reading a book, taking a warm bath, or practicing relaxation techniques such as deep breathing or meditation.

- Create a sleep-friendly environment by keeping your bedroom cool, dark, and quiet. Invest in a comfortable mattress and pillows that provide proper support. Consider using blackout curtains and white noise machines to block out external disturbances.

- The blue light emitted by electronic devices can interfere with your body's production of melatonin, a hormone that regulates sleep. Limit screen time at least an hour before bedtime to promote a more natural sleep-wake cycle.

- Be careful of consuming large meals, caffeine, and nicotine close to bedtime. These substances can disrupt sleep and make it more difficult to fall asleep or stay asleep throughout the night.

Healthy Diet

Maintaining a healthy diet plays a significant role in phobia recovery by influencing both physical and mental well-being. Nutrient-dense foods provide the necessary building blocks for neurotransmitters and hormones that regulate mood and stress response, contributing to emotional stability crucial for overcoming phobias.

A balanced diet, rich in fruits, vegetables, lean proteins, and whole grains, supports overall brain health and cognitive function, enhancing the effectiveness of therapeutic interventions such as cognitive-behavioral therapy (CBT). Additionally, stable blood sugar levels from a well-rounded diet can help manage anxiety symptoms often associated with phobias. Hydration is equally vital, as dehydration can exacerbate stress and negatively impact cognitive performance. Integrating a nutritious diet into phobia recovery fosters a holistic approach that addresses both physical and psychological aspects, promoting resilience and optimal conditions for the therapeutic process.

You can follow the following tips for a well-balanced diet:

- One key tip for maintaining a healthy diet is to focus on balanced meal planning. Include a variety of nutrient-dense foods from all food groups – fruits, vegetables, whole grains, lean proteins, and healthy fats. This ensures that your body receives the essential vitamins, minerals, and macronutrients it needs for optimal functioning.

- Practice portion control to avoid overeating. Pay attention to serving sizes and listen to your body's hunger and fullness cues. Eating mindfully and savoring each bite can help prevent consuming excess calories while fostering a more mindful relationship with food.

- Stay well-hydrated by drinking an adequate amount of water throughout the day. Water is crucial for various bodily functions, including digestion, nutrient absorption, and temperature regulation. Consider water as your primary beverage choice and limit the intake of sugary drinks.

- Minimize the consumption of processed foods and foods high in added sugars. These items often lack essential nutrients and can contribute to weight gain and various health issues. Instead, choose whole, unprocessed foods that provide more nutritional value.

- Include a variety of colorful fruits and vegetables in your daily meals. Different colors indicate various phytonutrients, vitamins, and minerals that offer a range of health benefits. Aim to fill half your plate with vegetables and fruits to maximize nutritional intake.

- Practice mindful eating by paying attention to your eating habits and sensations. Avoid distractions like screens while eating and savor the flavors, textures, and aromas of your food. Mindful eating can help prevent overeating and promote a healthier relationship with food.

- Opt for healthier cooking methods such as grilling, steaming, baking, or sautéing, which preserve the nutritional content of foods. Limit the use of frying or cooking methods that involve excessive amounts of added fats.

- Incorporate sources of healthy fats, such as avocados, nuts, seeds, and olive oil, into your diet. These fats are essential for brain health, hormone production, and the absorption of fat-soluble vitamins.

- Become familiar with reading food labels to make informed choices. Pay attention to the ingredient list, nutritional content, and serving sizes. This helps you make healthier choices and avoid products with excessive additives, preservatives, or hidden sugars.

- Adopt a mindset of moderation rather than deprivation. Allow yourself occasional treats or indulgences while focusing on maintaining an overall balanced and nutritious diet. Striving for balance rather than strict restriction promotes a sustainable and positive approach to healthy eating.

Problem-Solving Skills

Effective problem-solving skills are another valuable coping mechanism. Instead of avoiding or denying problems, individuals with good coping mechanisms tackle issues head-on. They assess the situation, identify potential solutions, and take proactive steps to address challenges. This approach empowers individuals to navigate difficulties effectively and fosters a sense of control over their lives.

Developing effective problem-solving skills is crucial for navigating life's challenges and making informed decisions. Here are some helpful problem-solving skills explained in paragraphs:

- Analytical Thinking: Analytical thinking involves breaking down complex problems into smaller, more manageable parts. It requires the ability to examine situations critically, identify patterns, and understand the underlying factors contributing to the issue. This skill enables individuals to approach problems with a systematic and structured mindset, facilitating a more comprehensive understanding of the challenges at hand.

- Creativity and Innovation: Creativity and innovation involve thinking outside the box to generate novel solutions. This skill encourages individuals to explore unconventional ideas, perspectives, and approaches to problem-solving. By fostering a creative mindset, individuals can uncover unique solutions and adapt to changing circumstances, adding a dynamic element to their problem-solving repertoire.

- Effective Communication: Effective communication is a vital skill in problem-solving, as it allows individuals to articulate their thoughts, share ideas, and collaborate with others. Clear and concise communication facilitates a better understanding of the problem and encourages constructive dialogue, helping teams work collaboratively toward solutions.

- Decision-Making: Decision-making is an integral component of problem-solving. It involves evaluating various options, considering potential outcomes, and making informed choices. Developing sound decision-making skills requires weighing the pros and cons, assessing risks, and aligning choices with personal or organizational goals. Being decisive ensures progress and resolution in problem-solving processes.

- Time Management: Time management is essential for efficient problem-solving. It involves allocating time wisely, setting priorities, and organizing tasks in a way that maximizes productivity. Effective time management ensures that individuals can dedicate adequate attention to each aspect of the problem-solving process without feeling overwhelmed or rushed.

- Resilience and Adaptability: Resilience and adaptability involve the ability to bounce back from setbacks and adjust strategies when faced with unforeseen challenges. Building resilience enables individuals to navigate setbacks without losing focus, maintaining a positive attitude, and learning from experiences to enhance future problem-solving approaches.

- Collaboration and Teamwork: Collaboration and teamwork are crucial problem-solving skills, especially in complex and multifaceted issues. Working collaboratively with diverse perspectives allows for a holistic examination of the problem, leveraging the collective intelligence of a group. Effective collaboration fosters creativity, innovation, and a shared sense of responsibility for finding solutions.

- Critical Thinking: Critical thinking involves the ability to objectively evaluate information, assess the credibility of sources, and make reasoned judgments. This skill is fundamental in problem-solving as it helps individuals separate fact from opinion, identify biases, and approach problems with a rational and logical mindset. Critical thinking enhances the quality of decision-making and problem resolution.

- Emotional Intelligence: Emotional intelligence plays a role in problem-solving by fostering self-awareness and empathy. Individuals with high emotional intelligence can navigate interpersonal dynamics, understand others' perspectives, and manage their own emotions effectively. This skill contributes to successful collaboration, conflict resolution, and overall positive problem-solving outcomes.

- Continuous Learning: Continuous learning is a mindset that encourages individuals to seek new knowledge and skills. In problem-solving, a commitment to ongoing learning allows individuals to stay updated on relevant information, explore innovative approaches, and adapt to evolving circumstances. Embracing a learning mindset enhances problem-solving capabilities over time.

Coping for Your Future

Incorporating these good coping mechanisms into one's daily life contributes to emotional well-being, resilience, and the ability to face life's challenges with a positive mindset. Building a diverse toolkit of effective coping strategies enhances an individual's capacity to navigate stressors and promote overall mental health.

Chapter Eight

Advanced Coping Strategies

In the realm of conquering phobias, the power of visualization and imagery emerges as a beacon of hope. This transformative tool taps into the intricate workings of the mind, allowing individuals to navigate their fears with mental acuity. As readers delve into this aspect, they are guided through the profound impact of mental imagery on the fear response. Abstract anxieties are translated into tangible, manageable scenarios within the controlled landscape of one's imagination. Visualization acts as a bridge, enabling individuals to confront and reframe their fears, fostering a sense of empowerment in the face of once-intimidating stimuli.

Crafting Personal Scripts for Common Phobias

In the endeavor to overcome phobias, crafting personal scripts becomes a pivotal aspect of the journey. These scripts are not just written words; they are tailored narratives that resonate with the unique fears and challenges individuals face. This personalized approach transforms abstract anxieties into tangible scenarios within the controlled realm of one's imagination.

- Identifying Specific Fears: The first step in crafting a personal script is identifying the specific fears that need addressing. Whether it's the fear of heights, social situations, or confined spaces, a clear understanding of the targeted fear lays the foundation for a script that speaks directly to the individual's experience. This identification process enables the script to be a precise tool for tackling the core of the phobia.

- Creating a Vivid Mental Landscape: Once the fear is identified, the script takes shape by creating a vivid mental landscape. The language used should be evocative, drawing upon sensory details to make the imagined scenario as realistic as possible. This process helps individuals immerse themselves in the narrative, making the feared situation palpable within the confines of their mind.

- Progressive Exposure in Words: Crafting a personal script involves incorporating a progressive exposure approach. Start with a milder version of the feared scenario and gradually escalate the intensity. This allows individuals to engage with the script at a pace that aligns with their current comfort level, ensuring that the exposure is manageable and not overwhelming.

- Incorporating Cognitive Restructuring: Integrating cognitive restructuring into the script adds a layer of empowerment. As individuals confront their fears within the script, they are encouraged to challenge and reframe negative thoughts associated with the phobia. This cognitive component serves as a tool for reshaping perceptions and building a more positive mindset in the face of fear.

- Repetition and Gradual Desensitization: Repetition is key to the efficacy of personal scripts. By revisiting the script regularly, individuals undergo a process of gradual desensitization. The more familiar they become with the script, the less potent the fear response becomes over time. This repetition reinforces the idea that the feared scenario is manageable, ultimately contributing to the reduction of anxiety associated with the phobia.

- Seeking Professional Guidance: While crafting personal scripts can be a powerful self-help tool, it's essential to acknowledge that seeking professional guidance is valuable. Mental health professionals can provide insights into tailoring scripts effectively and offer support in navigating the emotional aspects of the exposure process. The collaboration between personal scriptwriting and professional guidance creates a comprehensive approach to phobia treatment.

Crafting personal scripts for phobias involves a thoughtful and individualized process. It empowers individuals to confront their fears within the realm of their imagination, gradually reshaping their relationship with the phobia. Through carefully constructed narratives, individuals embark on a journey of self-discovery and resilience, using the power of words to rewrite their narrative of fear.

Hypnotherapy for Phobias

Venturing into alternative avenues, the exploration extends into the domain of hypnotherapy. Hypnotherapy is not portrayed as a mystical or elusive practice but as a method that can access the subconscious mind and reframe deeply rooted fears. The narrative sheds light on the potential synergy between hypnotherapy and traditional exposure techniques. This integration offers a holistic perspective, showing that phobia treatment can benefit from the collaborative efforts of both established and alternative methodologies.

Principles of Hypnotherapy

At its core, hypnotherapy operates on the principle of accessing the subconscious mind to bring about positive changes in thoughts, feelings, and behaviors. Readers are introduced to the idea that the subconscious mind, the reservoir of our beliefs and emotions, can be harnessed to reframe deeply rooted fears. Understanding this principle lays the foundation for exploring the potential synergy between hypnotherapy and traditional exposure techniques.

Phobias often have roots in subconscious thought patterns and associations. Hypnotherapy becomes a means to directly address and modify these patterns by inducing a heightened state of focused attention and suggestibility. Hypnotherapy can uncover and reprogram these subconscious elements, offering a targeted approach to dismantling the foundations of phobias.

Hypnotherapy often works with other techniques. The integration of hypnotherapy with traditional exposure techniques is crucial. By combining the power of suggestion and focused attention achieved through hypnosis with gradual exposure to feared stimuli, individuals can potentially accelerate the process of desensitization. Practical insights into how hypnotherapy sessions can be structured to complement exposure therapy are provided, encouraging readers to view these approaches as mutually reinforcing.

Beyond addressing phobic responses, hypnotherapy is presented as a tool for unlocking resilience. The induced state of relaxation and heightened suggestibility can contribute to reducing overall anxiety levels, enhancing an individual's capacity to face fears with greater calmness and composure. The section explores how hypnotherapy sessions can be tailored to instill a sense of empowerment and self-efficacy, fostering a mindset conducive to overcoming phobias.

Hypnotherapy's potential synergy with cognitive strategies is unveiled, showcasing how it can complement efforts to challenge and reframe distorted thought patterns associated with phobias. By exploring and reshaping cognitive distortions during hypnotherapy sessions, individuals may experience a more profound and integrated transformation in their approach to feared situations.

Hypnotherapy is not a standalone solution but as part of a holistic approach to phobia treatment. Readers are encouraged to view hypnotherapy as a versatile tool that can be integrated into their personalized strategies for conquering fears. The chapter concludes by highlighting the empowering nature of hypnotherapy, emphasizing its potential to unlock the resilient core within individuals, paving the way for a life free from the constraints of irrational fears.

Insights into Neuro-Linguistic Programming (NLP)

Expanding the options available, we can turn the spotlight to Neuro-Linguistic Programming (NLP), showing valuable insights into how language and communication shape thought patterns and behaviors. Practical applications of NLP techniques offer additional tools to augment existing coping strategies. The emphasis is on the adaptability of NLP, making it a versatile approach that individuals can incorporate into their unique phobia conquering journey. By understanding the role of language in shaping perceptions, readers gain a nuanced perspective on how NLP can contribute to the transformative process of overcoming irrational fears.

Neuro-Linguistic Programming (NLP) is an approach to communication, personal development, and psychotherapy that originated in the 1970s. It was developed by Richard Bandler and John Grinder. NLP is based on the premise that there is a connection between neurological processes (neuro), language patterns (linguistic), and behavioral patterns that have been learned through experience (programming).

The core principles of NLP revolve around understanding how individuals perceive and interpret the world, and how these perceptions influence their thoughts, behaviors, and emotions. NLP practitioners believe that by identifying and modifying specific patterns of thought and behavior, individuals can achieve personal and professional growth.

NLP explores how individuals create mental representations of experiences through visual and auditory modalities. Readers delve into the significance of these representations in shaping perceptions of fear. Techniques for modifying these mental images and sounds are introduced, allowing individuals to reframe and diminish the intensity of phobic responses. By altering the sensory aspects associated with fear, NLP becomes a tool for restructuring the cognitive landscape and fostering resilience.

One of the key tenets of NLP revolves around the interplay between language and thought patterns. We consider how the language we use internally and externally influences our perceptions and responses. Recognizing and reframing limiting language patterns become essential components of using NLP to address phobias. By gaining control over language, individuals can reshape their thought processes, fostering a more positive and empowering mindset in the face of fear.

Anchoring, a fundamental technique in NLP, is a valuable tool for phobia conquering, designed to create associations between external stimuli and specific emotional or mental states. This process involves selecting a distinct anchor, such as a touch, gesture, or word, and pairing it with a desired emotional state or mindset. By applying the anchor at the peak of the targeted state and repeating the process, individuals can establish a connection between the anchor and the associated experience. Once set, the anchor can be intentionally activated to evoke the desired state, providing a tool for self-regulation and emotional management.

Neuro-Linguistic Programming (NLP) can be considered a useful tool for addressing phobias by leveraging its techniques to understand and modify patterns of thought and behavior. The anchoring technique in NLP, for instance, allows individuals to associate positive states with specific stimuli, aiding in the intentional shift from fear to calmness. Moreover, NLP's emphasis on language patterns, reframing, and cognitive restructuring aligns with therapeutic approaches commonly used in phobia treatment. By addressing the intricate connections between neurology, language, and behavior, NLP provides individuals with a framework to explore and reshape their responses to phobic triggers. While its effectiveness may vary among individuals, and scientific consensus on NLP remains debated, some find value in its principles and applications as part of a comprehensive approach to phobia recovery. As with any therapeutic technique, its use should be considered within the broader context of evidence-based practices and individual preferences.

Holistic Integration into Phobia Treatment

Holistic integration refers to the incorporation and seamless blending of various therapeutic techniques and strategies into a comprehensive framework. This approach recognizes that phobias are multi-faceted and may require a diverse set of tools to address the cognitive, emotional, and behavioral aspects of fear. By embracing a holistic perspective, individuals gain a more comprehensive and tailored toolkit for overcoming their phobias.

Holistic integration begins with understanding that phobias extend beyond the surface manifestations of fear. It acknowledges the interconnectedness of thoughts, emotions, behaviors, and physiological responses. Rather than isolating these components, a holistic approach views them as interconnected elements that influence and reinforce each other. This understanding forms the foundation for crafting a treatment plan that addresses the entirety of the individual's experience.

Behavioral techniques, such as exposure therapy and systematic desensitization, are integral components of holistic phobia treatment. These techniques are designed to modify and reshape behavioral responses to feared stimuli. Holistic integration involves aligning these behavioral approaches with cognitive strategies to create a synergistic effect. By combining exposure therapy with cognitive restructuring, individuals not only confront their fears but also challenge and reshape the thought patterns that contribute to the phobia.

Holistic integration recognizes the power of cognitive strategies in reshaping thought patterns associated with phobias. Understanding cognitive distortions and employing cognitive restructuring exercises becomes a parallel track to behavioral techniques. By addressing the cognitive aspect of phobias, individuals gain tools to challenge irrational thoughts and foster a more balanced and realistic mindset in the face of fear.

The holistic approach extends to advanced coping strategies, such as visualization, imagery, hypnotherapy, and Neuro-Linguistic Programming (NLP). These techniques are not viewed in isolation but as complementary tools that can augment the effectiveness of traditional approaches. Visualization and imagery, for instance, provide a mental landscape for confronting fears, while hypnotherapy and NLP offer alternative avenues for reshaping deeply rooted thought patterns.

Holistic integration acknowledges the profound connection between the mind and body. Techniques that nurture mental well-being, such as mindfulness and relaxation exercises, are woven into the treatment plan. Recognizing how thoughts and emotions influence physical responses, individuals are encouraged to embrace practices that contribute to overall mental and emotional equilibrium.

One of the core tenets of holistic integration is the customization of treatment plans. Recognizing that individuals are unique, treatment plans are tailored to align with personal preferences, comfort levels, and specific phobic triggers. This customization ensures that individuals receive a treatment plan that resonates with their individual journey, fostering a sense of ownership and engagement in the therapeutic process.

You don't have to go through the process alone. Holistic integration encourages collaboration with mental health professionals who specialize in phobia treatment. This collaborative approach ensures that individuals receive expert guidance in navigating the complexities of their phobias. Mental health professionals can offer insights into tailoring treatment plans, provide emotional support, and guide individuals through the intricacies of their unique phobic challenges.

In essence, holistic integration into phobia treatment involves recognizing the multifaceted nature of phobias and adopting an approach that addresses the diverse aspects of the individual's experience. By blending behavioral techniques, cognitive strategies, advanced coping strategies, and a focus on the mind-body connection, individuals embark on a holistic journey toward overcoming their phobias with a more comprehensive and tailored set of tools.

Chapter Nine

Maintaining Progress

Dealing with phobias isn't all about what you need to do now to make change. You also have to consider what you'll have to do going forward to maintain progress. This chapter acknowledges the reality that setbacks are an intrinsic part of the journey but reframes them as opportunities for growth. Setbacks can be transformative, propelling individuals toward greater strength. Moreover, the chapter provides practical tips for the long-term management of phobias and strategies to prevent complacency.

Navigating Setbacks: Turning Challenges into Triumphs

Part of life is setbacks, which is why you must learn to embrace setbacks with a nuanced perspective that transcends the surface-level understanding of what defines phobia recovery. Far more than insurmountable obstacles, setbacks are positioned as fertile grounds for profound learning and unparalleled personal growth. You have to cultivate a mindset that recognizes setbacks not as roadblocks but as dynamic opportunities for evolution.

We all make mistakes and do things that we wish we could have done differently, but that doesn't mean those mistakes should lead to defeat. By acknowledging setbacks, we can remember that our struggles are not isolated incidents but are interconnected threads in the tapestry of overcoming our fears and living a full life.

Take the time to reflect on what went wrong, identify areas for improvement, and extract lessons that can inform future actions. Use setbacks as a platform for innovation and adaptability, adjusting strategies and approaches based on the insights gained. Embrace challenges as chances to build resilience, enhance problem-solving skills, and fortify your determination. By reframing setbacks as stepping stones toward improvement rather than roadblocks, you can cultivate a mindset that turns adversity into a catalyst for continuous progress and success.

Importance of Persistence

If you want to address the setbacks in your life, you need to learn persistence. Persistence refers to the quality of continuing to pursue a goal or task despite facing challenges, obstacles, or setbacks. It involves determination, tenacity, and the ability to stay focused on one's objectives even in the face of difficulties. Persistent individuals exhibit resilience and maintain their efforts over time, displaying a strong work ethic and a refusal to be easily discouraged. Persistence often involves a combination of motivation, grit, and the willingness to learn from failures, enabling individuals to overcome adversity and ultimately achieve their desired outcomes.

One crucial element in nurturing persistence is setting realistic expectations. The journey to conquer phobias is not linear; it's a series of peaks and valleys. Recognize that progress may come in small increments, and each step forward, no matter how modest, is a victory. Celebrate these small wins, as they contribute to the overall narrative of persistence and resilience.

Keep your eye on the long-term goal. Persistence flourishes when fueled by a commitment to the broader journey. Remind yourself of the life you envision beyond your phobias. Visualize the freedom and fulfillment awaiting you. This mental image can be a powerful motivator, sustaining your persistence through the ups and downs of the phobia-conquering odyssey.

Persistence is not a fixed trait but a skill that can be cultivated and refined over time. By embracing your challenges and keeping long-term goal in focus, you can can foster a tenacious persistence that propels them towards a life liberated from the shackles of irrational fears.

Staying the Course: Long-Term Management and Prevention

While setbacks are a struggle, there's no obstacle so big that you'll be sent off course. Phobia recovery requires some level of long-term management because if you don't continue to take care of your mental health new or old phobias may creep into your life. It gets easier to manage over time, but you can never stop striving to improve and protect yourself from future harm from phobias.

Practical Tips for Long-Term Management

Long-term management of phobias requires a multifaceted approach that extends beyond immediate coping mechanisms. Regular self-assessment emerges as a cornerstone practice, providing you with a consistent gauge of your progress. Routinely reflecting on your journey allows for the identification of areas that may need additional attention, fostering a proactive mindset in the face of potential setbacks.

Revisiting exposure techniques introduced earlier in the phobia-conquering journey becomes an essential aspect of long-term management. Incorporating these techniques into daily life not only reinforces the strides made but also serves as a preemptive measure against regression. By weaving exposure techniques into the fabric of your ordinary routine, you can create a sustainable approach to managing their fears, preventing the re-emergence of debilitating anxieties.

Seeking support when needed is another practical tip for long-term phobia management. A robust support network, comprising friends, family, or support groups, can provide invaluable assistance during challenging times. You've already learned to build a support group, and now it is time to use that group! Opening up about fears and triumphs fosters a sense of connection and reminds individuals that they are not alone on their journey. The shared understanding within a support network acts as a buffer against isolation and reinforces the resilience needed for sustained progress.

By integrating these practices into daily life, you can develop a robust framework for enduring progress, fostering a mindset that transcends the immediate challenges posed by phobias and aligns with the vision of a life liberated from phobias.

Strategies to Prevent Complacency

As you make significant strides in your journey to overcome phobias, the potential for complacency may emerge, threatening your hard-earned progress. To prevent complacency from impeding recovery, it's crucial to adopt strategic measures that maintain momentum and promote ongoing growth.

One effective strategy is the establishment of new goals. By continually setting achievable yet challenging objectives, individuals create a forward-looking mindset that prevents stagnation. These goals can be incremental steps in conquering specific fears or broader aspirations related to personal development. The pursuit of new objectives instills a sense of purpose, fostering an environment where complacency struggles to take root.

Continual personal growth becomes a shield against complacency. Actively seeking opportunities for learning and self-improvement reinforces the idea that the journey is ongoing. This may involve exploring new coping mechanisms, participating in support groups, or embracing activities that foster resilience. The commitment to personal growth cultivates a mindset that is inherently resistant to complacency.

Preventing complacency in phobia recovery requires a proactive and dynamic approach. Setting new goals and prioritizing personal growth, are strategies that collectively form a resilient shield against the creeping threat of complacency. By implementing these measures, individuals ensure that their journey remains vibrant, purposeful, and continually moving towards a life liberated from the constraints of irrational fears.

Chapter Ten

Living Without Fear

As we step into the concluding chapter of this transformative journey, the narrative pivots towards the possibility of a life unburdened by fear. Chapter 8 serves as a beacon of inspiration. You have all the tools you need to recover from your phobia and start a path towards your dream life. The following anecdotes show how people have transformed their lives by challenging their phobias and facing their fears.

Growing and Developing After Phobias

Embracing Adventure After Agoraphobia: Susan, once confined by agoraphobia, gradually confronted her fear of open spaces. Through exposure therapy and the support of a trusted friend, she explored parks, and markets, and eventually traveled to bustling cities. Today, Susan lives a life filled with travel adventures, embracing the vastness of the world she once feared.

Thriving in Social Circles After Social Phobia: James, who battled social phobia, immersed himself in social activities to overcome his fear. Starting with small gatherings, he expanded his social network, eventually becoming a pivotal member of various communities. James now thrives in social circles, proving that a life without the constraints of social anxiety is not only possible but can be richly rewarding.

From Claustrophobia to Cave Exploration: Emma, once gripped by claustrophobia, decided to challenge her fear by exploring caves. With the guidance of an experienced guide, she ventured into underground spaces. The gradual exposure not only conquered her fear but ignited a passion for spelunking. Emma now explores intricate cave systems, showcasing that life without phobias can lead to unexpected and fulfilling pursuits.

Conquering the Fear of Water: David, who struggled with aquaphobia, enrolled in swimming classes to confront his fear. Overcoming the initial panic, he discovered a love for water activities. David now enjoys swimming, kayaking, and even scuba diving. His transformation from fearing water to embracing aquatic adventures highlights the profound impact of conquering specific phobias.

Public Speaking Mastery After Glossophobia: Linda, once paralyzed by glossophobia, decided to pursue a career in public speaking. Through practice, coaching, and exposure, she not only conquered her fear but became a sought-after speaker. Linda now empowers others to find their voices, illustrating that a life without the fear of public speaking is not only achievable but can lead to impactful contributions.

Freedom from Fear of Flying: Mark, who avoided air travel due to a fear of flying, faced his phobia head-on. Through a combination of therapy and gradual exposure, he now travels extensively by plane. Mark's story demonstrates that life without the limitations of a specific phobia opens doors to new experiences and opportunities.

These narratives illuminate the transformative power of overcoming phobias. Individuals like Susan, James, Emma, David, Linda, and Mark showcase that living fully without phobias is not merely a concept but a tangible reality. Each story is a testament to the resilience of the human spirit and the boundless possibilities that await when irrational fears no longer dictate the terms of one's life.

Paying It Forward: The Ripple Effect of Success

This part of the book looks beyond yourself. It's time for us to extend a heartfelt invitation to pay it forward. Beyond the personal triumphs meticulously explored in the preceding pages, the eBook emphasizes the profound impact of generosity. It encourages readers not only to bask in the glow of their own success but to become mentors, guiding lights for others who are setting foot on a similar path. The act of sharing success and knowledge emerges as a cornerstone, a selfless gesture that fuels the collective journey toward a life unbridled by fear.

Paying it forward is not merely a singular act; it is the initiation of a ripple effect—a cascade of inspiration and empowerment that stretches far beyond individual victories. With each shared success story, a ripple is cast into the vast sea of shared human experiences. This ripple, gentle yet profound, becomes a beacon for those navigating the shadows of their own fears. You can become part of this ripple and use your negative experiences to create positive changes

This eBook, through its emphasis on paying it forward, envisions the creation of a community bound by shared experiences and collective strength. As individuals extend their hands to uplift others, a network of support takes shape—an intricate web woven with threads of shared triumphs, lessons learned, and the enduring spirit of resilience.

The act of sharing success is not confined to the exchange of words or anecdotes; it is a profound demonstration of the transformative power that resides in each personal triumph. Success stories, when shared, cease to be mere narratives—they become beacons of hope, roadmaps for others navigating the tumultuous terrain of phobias. You need to start thinking of your story as a success story. Even if you aren't free of your phobia, you are still working towards liberation, and that's a huge step.

When you feel more established in your recovery, you are encouraged to step into the role of mentor, offering not only guidance but unwavering support to those still finding their way. The collective strength of shared knowledge becomes a guiding force, illuminating the path toward living without fear for those who might be struggling in the darkness.

The ripple effect generated by paying it forward amplifies the impact of personal triumphs. Each shared success story is not just a drop in the ocean; it creates waves of inspiration and empowerment that reverberate across the community. The cumulative strength of these waves becomes a force to be reckoned with, dismantling the barriers of fear one ripple at a time.

Envisioning a Future Without Fear

CONQUERING PHOBIAS

As we stand at the threshold of a future without fear, this concluding chapter serves as more than just a reflection; it becomes a wellspring of inspiration. Readers, having absorbed the uplifting anecdotes woven through the preceding chapters, are now poised on the precipice of their own transformative journey. The collective wisdom shared becomes the wind beneath their wings, propelling them forward into the unknown with newfound courage.

The vision of a future without fear takes tangible form within these pages. It is not a distant mirage but a palpable destination within reach. Fueled by the stories of those who have navigated the same path, readers are invited to envision a life unencumbered by the constraints of irrational fears. The anecdotes become more than tales; they are blueprints for possibility, lighting the way through the darkness of uncertainty.

Embedded within the vision of a fear-free future is the powerful concept of empowerment through teaching. This eBook underscores that teaching is not merely an act of imparting knowledge but a transformative journey in itself. As individuals share their experiences, triumphs, and insights, they become architects of their own empowerment. Teaching becomes a conduit for reinforcing personal progress, a dynamic force that propels individuals beyond the boundaries of their fears.

Teaching becomes a two-fold journey—one of giving and receiving. As individuals generously share their knowledge and triumphs, they extend a gift to others who may be just embarking on their own odyssey. Simultaneously, the act of teaching becomes a profound reinforcement of personal triumphs. In the process of empowering others, individuals find themselves strengthened, solidifying their own resilience and growth.

The act of sharing knowledge becomes a sacred exchange, a passing of the torch from one individual to another. The insights gained from personal victories, setbacks, and the overall journey contribute to a collective reservoir of wisdom. This shared knowledge becomes a beacon, guiding not only those currently grappling with phobias but also future seekers of a life unburdened by fear.

Empowering others through teaching becomes a catalyst for continued personal growth. It is a reminder that the journey toward conquering phobias is not a solitary one. By contributing to the growth of others, individuals perpetuate their own upward trajectory. The act of empowerment is a dynamic force, propelling individuals forward on the path of resilience and self-

Chapter Eleven

Conclusion

In the culmination of this transformative journey toward conquering phobias, it becomes evident that the power to overcome irrational fears lies within the grasp of each individual. This eBook has served as a guide, offering not only insights into the intricacies of phobias but also a roadmap for reclaiming control over one's life. As we stand at the conclusion of these pages, it is our sincerest hope that you, the reader, now possess not only a profound understanding of the psychological underpinnings of phobias but also a rich toolbox of strategies to combat them. The exploration of the psychology behind phobias in Chapter 1 has provided a foundational understanding, laying bare the roots and manifestations of these often crippling anxieties. Armed with insights into the brain's role in fear response and the identification of specific phobias through self-assessment tools, readers are equipped with the knowledge needed to embark on their personal journey of transformation.

As we draw the final curtain on this exploration into phobias, let it be a proclamation—a testament to the indomitable human spirit and the unwavering pursuit of liberation. The journey embarked upon within these pages has been one of introspection, resilience, and profound transformation, unveiling the hidden corridors of the mind where fears take root.

The stories shared, strategies unveiled, and insights gained collectively form a tapestry of triumph over phobias. Real-life narratives have illuminated the path forward, proving that liberation from the shackles of irrational fears is not a distant dream but an achievable reality. Each individual who embarks on this journey contributes to a collective victory, redefining the narrative of what is possible.

The acknowledgment of setbacks becomes not a concession of defeat but a recognition of the inherent challenges in the pursuit of conquering phobias. Real-life stories have shown that setbacks need not derail the journey but can become stepping stones toward greater strength. Navigating the peaks and valleys, individuals forge ahead, resilient in the face of adversity.

Envisioning a life free from the constraints of phobias is not a mere utopian vision but a tangible destination within reach. The concluding chapters have invited readers to embrace this new dawn, inspired by real-life success stories and propelled by the transformative power of paying it forward. The odyssey toward living without fear is not just a possibility—it is an inevitability for those who dare to take the steps.

The toolkit provided, ranging from exposure therapy and cognitive strategies to coping mechanisms and advanced techniques, is not just a set of tools but a guide for the ongoing journey. It empowers individuals to navigate the complexities of their fears, fostering a sense of agency and autonomy in the face of phobic challenges.

This book has been a lantern in the darkness, illuminating the mind's pathways and revealing that the journey to conquer phobias is not a solitary endeavor. It is a shared exploration, a collective uprising against the shadows that seek to constrain our potential for joy and fulfillment.

As we part ways, may this book linger as a companion throughout your journey, its pages echoing with the encouragement to continue the journey toward a life liberated from irrational fears. The journey does not end with the last page but extends into the realms of your daily life, where each moment becomes an opportunity to apply the insights gained.

The freedom to live without fear is a treasure waiting to be discovered. May you carry the wisdom gained from these pages as a torch, illuminating the path toward your own liberation. The path toward a life free from the grip of irrational fears is a journey worth taking, and the freedom you seek is yours to embrace. Don't put off recovery any longer. Start today and seek to use your changing self to improve the world and your overall well-being.

www.ingramcontent.com/pod-product-compliance
Lightning Source LLC
LaVergne TN
LVHW051952060526
838201LV00059B/3608